The Art of Food

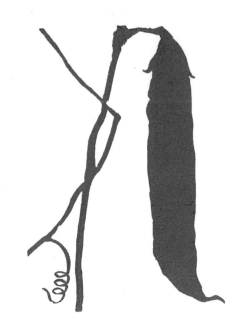

The Art of Food

By SHIRLEY ABBOTT

Edited by IRWIN GLUSKER

OXMOOR HOUSE, INC · BIRMINGHAM

THE ART OF FOOD

Copyright © by Oxmoor House, Inc.
Book Division of The Progressive Farmer Company
Publisher of *Southern Living*®, *Progressive Farmer*®,
and *Decorating & Craft Ideas*® magazines
P.O. Box 2463, Birmingham, Alabama 35202

Eugene Butler *Chairman of the Board*
Emory Cunningham *President and Publisher*
Vernon Owens, Jr. *Senior Vice President*
Roger McGuire *Executive Vice President*

Published by Oxmoor House, Inc., under the direction of:

Don Logan *Vice President and General Manager*
Gary McCalla *Editor, Southern Living*
John Logue *Editor-in-Chief*
Jean Wickstrom *Foods Editor*

Conceived and produced by Duobooks Inc., New York:

Irwin Glusker *Editorial and Design Director*
Henry Horowitz *Production Director*
Margaret Riggs Buckwalter *Picture Editor*
Cela Wright *Layout and Project Coordinator*
Lilyan Glusker *Copy and Traffic*

Library of Congress Catalog Number: 79-83704
ISBN: 0-8487-0497-5

Manufactured in the United States of America

First printing 1979

Contents

Page one: Walter Stein, Peas, 1956, woodblock print from A Common Botany
Page two: Winslow Homer, The Dinner Horn, *1875, The Detroit Institute of Arts*
Above: Ellsworth Kelly, Artichokes, *1961, Museum of Modern Art*

The Art of Food

By SHIRLEY ABBOTT

The oldest paintings that survive on earth were made some seventeen thousand years ago in the dark caves and caverns at Lascaux, in what is now southern France. Although the painters can be classified accurately as cave people, they were far from being beetle-browed Flintstone types—both physically and mentally, they were, in fact, much like us. And what subject did they choose for their murals?

Food. Not something served up on a china platter, to be sure, but food on the hoof—the giant wild cattle, the bison, the deer that roamed the sparse pastures of southern Europe toward the end of the last Ice Age. These talented cave dwellers portrayed the animals they depended upon for their steaks and chops as well as for leather and skins. Yet difficult as the hunt and kill may have been (and imagine butchering an entire cow with nothing but a stone knife), they found time to turn the game not only into something edible but into something beautiful. For the wall paintings of these splendid animals are in many ways as accomplished and strong as any art ever made.

Food, usually in the form of a dependable grain supply, is the economic foundation of civilized life – the basis of a thousand other essentials: the fire on the hearth; the temple and the palace; the winds in the sails of merchant ships; the paving blocks in the city streets; the vineyards; the well-set table; the written word and the whole agglomeration of ideas and objects and habits that through the ages has come to signify civilization. The intelligence and skill of a people may help a nation become civilized. Without food, however, intelligence and skill don't go very far: without a reliable supply of grain – the basic foodstuff – our lives become, ironically, nothing more than a struggle to get hold of it. We then have no time for the pleasures and passions of civilized life – art, good food, or anything else.

Civilization began when mankind gave up hunting for a living and started to depend on a steadier, if less exhilarating, means of livelihood – farming. For reasons that no one can explain, in various times and places – perhaps as long ago as seven thousand years in Persia and Egypt and other Biblical lands – people who had lived for millenia as hunters and gatherers, feeding on the flesh of wild animals and whatever they could pick off bushes and trees, decided to stop hunting and start farming. It has been said that hunting was not a bad way of life. The story of the Garden of Eden may even reflect the simplicity and the social equality of the prehistoric hunting days. And, if so, it may indeed have been Eve who brought Eden to an end – agriculture was probably a feminine invention. In those days, it was undoubtedly women who harvested the wild fruits and grains, and perhaps it occurred to them that they could grow their own fruit trees and plant vegetable gardens. In any case, people gradually settled down to grow their own food, learning in the process how to cultivate and plough, how to irrigate and fertilize, how to make the good earth yield. To us, it may appear elementary, but it was a revolutionary invention that sets even the modern computer in the shade.

These fledgling farmers multiplied. We call it the population explosion, and it continues unabated to this day. The village that managed to grow enough grain to feed itself year-round usually prospered and grew larger. As there were more hands to produce food, more food was needed. As soon as there was enough grain to store up against a famine, granaries were built and cities grew. When there was enough grain to export, caravans were organized and ships were built. At first, these ships sailed close to shore – the open sea was terrifying to the early sailors. Eventually, these same ships might travel back to port with their hulls full of spices, amber, furs, cotton cloth – for one of the earliest trade routes went from what is now the Persian Gulf to present-day India, and it was in India that cotton was first grown. Soon, all because of grain, a leisured class arose, with the means and the taste to command all kinds of beautiful things – jewels and clothes and perfumes, not to mention well-cooked food served on attractive dishes. Not everybody was obliged to be a farmer anymore. For good or for ill, the old equality of Eden (which, after all, may have been only a dream) was at an end.

But the whole emerging edifice, however glittering and complex it became, stood or fell by food. And what was true in the time of Ashurbanipal is still true. Even in this day of high technology, when Americans worry a great deal more about petroleum than they do about wheat, the wealth of nations depends not only on their oil fields but on their wheat fields – those amber waves of grain that we used to sing about in school.

If food is the foundation of the economy and the basis of civilized life, it is also at the heart of that life—one of its delights, preoccupations, and ornaments. Food is part of religion. All religions have their feast days; many have rituals involving bread and wine. Food is part of social life and business life. To set a lavish table has always been one of the surest ways to impress one's friends and overwhelm one's adversaries: the business lunch was undoubtedly invented along with the business deal. Food is part of dying—at least for the survivors. Funerals have always been occasions for feasts—even today, a covered dish or a baked ham is one of the first things that neighbors bring to a bereaved household. Food is part of power—when kings and presidents assemble, do they ever forget to sit down at the banquet table? Food is part of love— fraternal, familial, conjugal, romantic, or diversionary. And as the briefest glance through these pages will reveal, it is and always has been part of art.

The Romans adopted the custom of reclining while dining from the classic Greeks, their mentors in these matters. The dinner party above is from a 4th century B.C. Greek krater (one is shown on the floor at left), a vessel used for mixing wine and water. National Museum, Naples

The uses that artists have made of food are as varied as food itself. Sometimes they treat it casually and obliquely, almost indirectly: a few figs on the table at some ancient Etruscan banquet, a stone relief of women baking bread in the ovens of a Roman kitchen, some fish in Simon Peter's net as Jesus calls him to discipleship (page 28), burly peasants lolling in a glorious golden field of wheat (page 16). Sometimes food is simply an accessory in a scene of good living—as in the earthy rendering by Frans Hals of drinkers in a tavern at Shrovetide (page 64), or Bonnard's light-drenched breakfast room (page 20). Sometimes it is highly abstract, refined out of edibility, as in the preciously wrought Easter egg (page 60) by the famous nineteenth-century Russian enamelist Fabergé. Sometimes food is the centerpiece and sole subject of a painting, as in Vincent van Gogh's stolid picture of potatoes in a yellow dish (page 68) or in Edouard Manet's luminescent, lusciously realistic treatment of fat oysters laid bare in their shells (page 76).

The Egyptians were among the first civilized people to depict food in their paintings and sculpture. They were also among the first to build a great power based on grain. The pyramids are in one sense merely Pharaoh's idea of a fitting way to spend the excess wealth created by bumper crops of wheat. The pyramids served as grandiose tombs, elaborately decorated and fitted out with the necessities of death. Since food was part of the baggage that a foresighted traveler carried with him to the next world, the pyramids were filled with it. Some of it was real—for example, the almonds and dates and fruits that have survived, in petrified form, to this day. Some of it was painted on the walls—fish in the sea and okra on the bush, onions and figs, fat geese, wheat, bread, grapes, game birds, and all the other good things that the Egyptians ate, for they were fine cooks and enthusiastic eaters, as well as dedicated beer drinkers. Their finest banquets were often held when some deceased dignitary was sealed up in his tomb.

The spirit of conviviality surrounding eating, rather than the food itself, is what most often engaged the talents of the Etruscan or Roman painter. Banquets and feasts—again, some-times in connection with a funeral—were frequent subjects in ancient art, though the fun of the occasion and the splendid dress of the participants are usually more impressive to our eyes than either the high spiritual purpose or the eatables. The average Roman-style banquet was an all-male affair (except for what might be politely called dancing girls) that consisted of two parts:

first, too much to eat, followed rapidly by too much to drink. It was an exercise in horizontal gluttony. The tradition of the groaning board, in life as in art, certainly did not die out with the Romans, but it gradually became somewhat less gross as people learned to sit up at table and not eat themselves into a stupor.

Banquets always seem to call for some kind of commemoration—even today, we bring in photographers. When medieval painters re-created scenes of sociability, they usually glossed them over with a religious meaning. If a medieval miniaturist shows a feast in progress, it is likely to be on a Biblical theme. Christ turning the water into wine at the marriage feast at Cana, Belshazzar's banquet, at which a mysterious hand wrote a warning on the wall, even the Last Supper, were occasions for the artist to show people at table—usually set with the utensils and victuals of the artist's own day.

But for many centuries food remained an almost incidental subject, like most of the trappings and appurtenances of everyday existence. Even in the Renaissance, when painters began to take pleasure in showing in exquisite sensuous detail a lace collar, say, or a ruff (as in the painting of the Cobham family on page 52) or the folds of a gorgeously betasseled mantle (as in the *Primavera*, page 112), food and flowers and other commonplace objects of everyday existence were hardly ever the central subject of a painting. Then gradually—it is impossible to say when or why, but sometime during the seventeenth century (at the time, incidentally, when the American colonies were being founded)—a subtle change took place in public taste, or at least in the preoccupation of artists.

While the painters of the Middle Ages most typically worked within the cramped dimensions of an altar panel, the painters of the Renaissance, by contrast, were more often confronted with the wall of a chapel or a palace. But little by little these forms began to be replaced by something more private and more manageable: a piece of canvas stretched on a frame and set up on an easel. A painter was no longer invariably obliged to labor in a cathedral or the house of a great prince. He could work in his own studio. He could make as good a living painting merchants as he could painting madonnas.

Because of this new autonomy, artists began to seek out the homely things of ordinary life—for their own sake and value, not merely as props in some pious landscape. The secular began to catch up with the sacred as the proper concern of art. And like the lens of a movie camera focussing on one figure in a crowd and then moving slowly in for a closeup, the painter began to focus on the small felicities of household life, and a form of painting called the still-life was born.

This did not happen at a definable moment, but it may have begun in the Netherlands and in Flanders, where by the end of the fifteenth century artists had some practice at showing the interiors of middle-class homes, along with their well-dressed occupants. The Flemish master Jan van Eyck knew how to study the small object. His famous portrait of *Giovanni Arnolfini and his Wife*, done in 1434, already has elements of the still-life in it. The mirror in the background, for example, and the gleaming chandelier are so well painted that they almost upstage the dour Arnolfini and his timid bride.

In any case, the still-life eventually came to be one of the most appreciated forms of art. It is usually a study of a selection of perfectly ordinary things, carefully arranged on a tabletop, painted with great attention to detail—an excellent showcase for the painter's virtuosity. The still-life catches its subject exactly in the light of the moment, and one of its pleasures has always

Giovanni Arnolfini and his Wife,
*painted in 1434 by Jan van Eyck.
National Gallery, London*

Contemporary and compatriot of Rembrandt, Jan Davidsz de Heem brought the Dutch still-life to its effulgent height. In this relatively small Still Life, *painted on a wooden panel, de Heem displays the same virtuosity he brought to his more sizable, and occasionally overwrought, work. The Metropolitan Museum of Art*

been its ability to fool the eye. "How real it looks!" the viewer exclaims. And the centerpiece of the still-life, more often than not, is something to eat.

Something to eat: peaches and grapes, tumbling over the sides of bowls and baskets, suddenly attracting a loving eye and a skillful hand to transfer their goodness to canvas. Fish glistening with seawater on wooden tables, wine in crytsalline glasses rendered to a shatterable thinness. In thousands of paintings, over the course of many years, the art of the kitchen tabletop slowly came into its own. It was brought to one kind of scintillating perfection in France in the last years of the nineteenth century and the first years of our own, by such painters as Manet, Renoir, Degas, and particularly, Cézanne (page 40).

If ever an artist took a relatively modest genre and turned it into a vehicle for master-pieces, it was Paul Cézanne. He lived for years, almost as a recluse, in the South of France, not very far from where those first cave painters had worked, though he knew nothing of them. He hardly ever sold enough of his work to pay for paint and canvas, and he died in 1906, unknown to the world at large. But he could set a few onions or apples and a bottle of wine on a tablecloth and paint them so that they possessed the solidity of mountains and the individuality of the human face. In the portraits he made using his wife as a model, and in the illimitable land-scapes he created out of the gentle mountains of Provence, neither the woman nor the mountains have any greater dignity or mass than the apples and onions of the still-lifes. The solidity of the earth is in them. Cézanne was not the first or the last painter to study the contours of everyday things, but his way of looking at a few pieces of fruit on a table endows these all too transient commodities with a reassuring permanence.

Dozens of American painters, too, have made their contributions to the culinary museum. The joys of food and of art have proved as inseparable in the New World as in the Old. Nowhere is this more clearly to be seen than in what we call folk art—for example, the tavern sign (page 128), which now symbolizes a way of life gone for good. And among the pictures here are other American paintings, made originally for various other uses, that are lovely and joyful in different ways: the glowing still-life by Raphaelle Peale on the jacket of this book, the young woman sounding the dinner horn opposite the title page, the single delicate *Tomato* (page 96), and Wayne Thiebaud's neat sandwich, forever fresh beneath its skewered olives—a light snack for the eyes (page 116).

Food is not only a perennial subject for fine art. Cuisine and its attendant pleasures are in themselves an art. Good cooking uses many of the same methods and provides many of the same rewards as painting and sculpture. Cooking cannot be done without experienced, knowing hands: the thumb that steadies the fruit in the path of the paring knife, the heel of the hand that presses out a pastry crust, the fingers that pat the top of a rising loaf and detect whether it is done. Cooking, more than any other kind of human inventiveness, is rooted in our daily lives. Not everyone has the talent to be a famous painter, nor for that matter a famous cook. But cooking is, after all, a most accessible art, requiring only a modest aptitude, along with great patience and a set of tastebuds still capable of savoring something besides TV dinners and pizza. Not only is cooking a learnable, do-able art, but it is a very necessary one, and its emotional rewards are great.

In *Remembrance of Things Past*, Marcel Proust recalled Françoise, the cook at his great-aunt's house, who spent most of her waking hours in the kitchen. But Françoise was not a drudge. She lived, wrote Proust reverentially, "in a ferment of creativity." Her weekly visit to the market, where she selected the joints of beef or veal that she later transformed into delicious concoctions for the family table, were, Proust thought, momentous journeys. They were to Françoise every bit as serious as Michelangelo's pilgrimages to the mountains of Carrara for the precisely right piece of marble to haul back to Florence or Rome.

The American cook, rummaging through plastic trays of hamburger at the local supermarket, may hardly share the fine emotional frenzy of Michelangelo (who at least got paid for his work) or the creative élan of Françoise. Yet it is not too far-fetched to say that even at the rummaging-through-the-supermarket stage—and beyond—some artistry has to come into play. The recent burgeoning of the small specialty foods store, butcher shop, cheese store, and herbarium is the surest sign that American cooks are disillusioned with the supermarket as the be-all and end-all in grocery shopping.

A discriminating eye is the beginning in cuisine, but other talents are needed as well. The culinary classic, of course, like a great work of art, is often the creation of one cook working alone—slowly making changes and refining. It may also be the result of a great leap of imagination on the part of a *cuisinier* unafraid to put his very life on the line. French cooking, not too surprisingly, provides an example or two of such dedication: in 1671, King Louis XIV's maître d'hôtel, Jean François Vatel, ran himself through with a sword after botching a royal banquet. More recently, a French chef shot himself after the Guide Michelin took away one of his stars.

But while heroic melodrama à la française may occasionally be seen in the kitchen, the exigencies of everyday life—even hard times—are just as important in cuisine. Great national traditions, and in particular the French, are based on an accumulation of regional habits and experience. This is simply the product of a lot of cooks in a lot of kitchens taking the raw materials of the countryside—whatever they can lay hands on—and turning them into good things to eat, stretching the materials and their imaginations as far as possible.

This means that a cook—usually, but not necessarily, a woman—knows something about how fruit and vegetables are grown and how to handle a bucket of new milk and what to do with a fresh-killed piece of meat. She has a nose that catches the scent of things and an eye for color, as well as a strong intuitive sense of quality—of what is poor, mediocre, and fine. She has the talent not merely to make something out of something but to make something out of nothing. She has a will to conserve, preserve, and save. This may involve grinding a few unlikely cuts of pork into sausage and seasoning it well, or taking the trouble to toss some bones into a stockpot, or inventing some way to pickle and preserve every last edible substance that can be harvested from the kitchen garden.

Few American cooks today can come up to these formidable standards—how could we? Many of us are already one or two generations away from the farm—or from the same traditions of frugality that ruled urban kitchens in an earlier day. Besides, most recipes today actively encourage the cook to throw things out ("trim all the fat," "take eight egg yolks"). But paradoxically, in this day of plenty, the sense of frugality that previous generations knew so well ought to be part of any good regional tradition of cooking. Few cooks these days have time to keep the stockpot boiling or the skill to make sausage or the inclination to soak a bushel of cucumbers in brine. But most of us have at least a few family traditions that we can hang on to or resurrect before it is too late. And the cook who *will* take the trouble to make the most of what she has or, once in a while, start from scratch is probably going to produce something better than ordinary.

And yet the roots of a great national tradition of cookery are hard to locate, however skilled its individual cooks may be. Nobody has ever quite figured out why France and China have developed distinctive and endlessly delicious cuisines based on an enormous repertory of ingredients, while England and America (so far) have not. For when this country was first settled, in the seventeenth and eighteenth centuries, the potential for a brilliant new way of cooking and eating existed.

In the first place, there was an astonishing new catalogue of raw materials. Instead of the wheat and oats and barley of the British Isles, there was corn. Instead of mutton, there was pork and when the cattle business got under way, in the nineteenth century, there were prodigious amounts of high-quality beef. There were new kinds of flat beans, and peas, and wonderful varieties of squash, including pumpkins—all cultivated by the Indians. White potatoes, which originated in South America, had already been transported to Europe, but yams were the typical North American tuber. The tomato, too, was an American native—though most of the early settlers were convinced that it was poisonous and refused to touch it. In addition, there were fish, shellfish, and wild game—not in strange new varieties but in overwhelming quantities, and all free.

Also, as time went on, dramatic new cultural influences came to bear on the European colonists, particularly in the South. The first of these was the Indian. Not many of us realize today that, among the original inhabitants of America's East Coast, the southern Indians in the early nineteenth century were referred to as the Five Civilized Tribes. They were skilled farmers as well as hunters. The Cherokees, who lived in the hill country of the Carolinas, and in Georgia, Alabama, and Tennessee, were particularly advanced. From them, the new settlers surely learned all the techniques of dealing with corn: how to plant it; grind it into meal; turn it into hominy and make cakes of it, either baked in an oven or simply fried on a stone—the pones and hoecakes and johnnycakes that have been part of Southern cooking ever since. They learned, too, the trick of cooking roasting-ears in their shucks, and the cultivation of beans and squash. Some people believe that the Southern custom of cooking vegetables for half a day in a big pot seasoned with animal fat was picked up from the Indians. Succotash, as the name reveals, was an Indian dish. The colonists may have had apprehensions about their Indian neighbors, but they were wise to adopt some of the Indians' ways.

The second new culture that confronted the whites was, of course, the African—most often, but certainly not exclusively, in the Southern states. Though the blacks were brought to this country unwillingly, deprived of all their former possessions and shorn of even their native languages and religions, they surely did not forget what they had eaten and how they had cooked it. Nor were the foodstuffs of America entirely new to them. Yams, for one thing, had long ago been transported to West Africa and had become a staple there. Chicken, beans, and peanuts were familiar, too. As African men and women took their places in the kitchens of the plantation South, their customs and tastes must surely have been evident. Moreover, in their own cabins they cooked to suit themselves. Many slaves grew and preserved their own food, rather than depend on rations handed out from the plantation house. They planted yams and field peas and corn; they raised hogs (once the mainstay of all Southerners, regardless of race or class); they fished or foraged. They shot possums and squirrels and rabbits—for they did have guns to hunt with, despite the law in some states forbidding blacks to carry firearms.

Like the Indians (and in Colonial times some slaves *were* Indians), the blacks were experts

A picture of life in Secotan, a well-ordered Indian village in coastal North Carolina, was engraved around 1590 by de Bry from John White's watercolor. Identifiable crops are tobacco (E) at the head of the road; corn, guarded by a human scarecrow (F and G); and what appear to be pumpkins in the narrow patch to the right of the road. Hunters pursue deer at the edge of the forest, upper left. New York Public Library

at the casserole — the meal that stewed all day in one pot. They had to be. They lacked not only the utensils but often the time to prepare things separately.

The contribution of the blacks to Southern cooking may at best be an arguable point. In one respect the slaves were masters — masters at making do — for thrift is the essence of soul food. The tops of turnips, the intestines of pigs, wild plants like poke sallet were not beneath the notice of the black cook. But the same may be said of backwoods white cooking, for the Southern pioneer in the hill country was hard-pressed, too. And after the Civil War all Southerners, with few exceptions, shared the bitter culture of do-without.

Yet the black gift was always felt in Southern history. At one ravenous moment after Sherman's march through Georgia, as depicted in *Gone With The Wind*, Scarlett O'Hara summons up a recollection of a well-laden dinner table at Tara: "Rolls, corn muffins, biscuits, and waffles, dripping butter, all at one meal. Ham at one end of the table and fried chicken at the other, collards swimming richly in pot liquor irridescent with grease, snap beans in mountains on brightly flowered porcelain, fried squash, stewed okra, carrots in cream sauce thick enough to cut. . . ." Though Scarlett surely would not have cared to know the ethnic origins of the cooking at Tara, everything she remembered, except the yeast rolls and the creamed carrots, was soul food.

*B*ut whatever the culinary dreams and promise of America may have been — and one dream was to feed every citizen better than marginally — many critics, both natives and visitors, have, for the past two hundred years, been tough on American cooking. In his wonderfully engaging work *Eating in America*, Waverley Root observes that "the United States, in the exercise of 'its inalienable right...to the Pursuit of Happiness' might very well have seized the opportunity to declare its independence of the English cuisine." For, as Mr. Root goes on to say, the colonists, whatever their country of origin, took the staggering new repertory of ingredients and methods and stubbornly re-created, as nearly as they could, the dishes they had grown up on.

The very number of all those newly landed cooks (and it is arguable that their objective was mere replication), at work in different places, in different seasons, with widely varying ethnic derivations and levels of prosperity, has produced a gastronomic kaleidoscope that hardly stands still long enough to be judged. It is very difficult to focus on a moveable feast.

Until recently, the best cooking in this country — especially in the South — has less often been found in restaurants than in homes, hidden from the eyes of practicing food critics and the yearnings of questing travelers, which may have given rise to some of the carping. Nevertheless, barring an excess of bad luck, it has always been possible to eat well in the cities of the South — New Orleans, Charleston, Galveston, Memphis, Louisville, Mobile, for starters.

However, in recent years chain restaurants and fast-food operations have multiplied, meeting a demand that one can only concede exists. In some ways, the fast-food purveyors are better than the greasy-spoon roadside diners of twenty years ago. In those days, perhaps, you might more easily have been able to tell where you were by what you were eating. On the gulp-and-run level, there might have been a greater difference between what the traveler found in a roadside eatery on the way to Pamlico Sound and what he found on the way to Puget Sound. The differences still do exist, but you have to get off the Interstate to find them. What you find may be as simple as a perfect orange bought at a stand in central Florida or as complex as a stately Creole dinner in New Orleans. The point is that you can still eat something wonderful in one place that can never be *that good* anywhere else.

A widely traveled friend of mine is an avid fish eater. He describes with joy stopping at a tin-roofed shack at the westerly end of Marathon, Florida, just before the road leaves Key Vaca to make its next leap over the blue-green water toward Key West. A homemade sign promised "Fried Fish & Cold Beer," both of which he ordered. The fish turned out to be a generous wedge of just-caught grouper, deep-fried to glowing bronze as my friend watched over his cutting-cold beer. The fixin's were appropriate and equally fresh. For all this, he got change back from a five-dollar bill. He resumed his journey with a prayer of thanks on his lips.

Several years later, that same friend, lunching in a space–age hotel in downtown Washington, D.C., responded to a menu blurb for "Fish of the Day—The Fresh Local Catch." Remembering the unfailing quality of the seafood in the good, sawdusty fish restaurants of another part of town—restaurants that got their fish fresh from nearby Chesapeake Bay—he ordered the special. The "fresh local catch" turned out to be Alaska King Crab.

*S*o we win some and we lose some, but we have certainly won more than we have lost. In the years since World War II, a momentous change has come about in the way food is grown and distributed in the United States. And while this mechanism does produce the waxen winter tomato and "fresh local" Alaska King Crab, another result is that the staples of our diet are uniformly available across the land, with enough left over to export abroad.

With this gigantic apparatus in place and functioning smoothly, something good is beginning to happen. All over the country—not just in big cities—there is a new interest in good cooking and good wines, in cookbooks, in workable, livable kitchens, in entertaining. Not the once-a-year catered affair of yesterday, but a good dinner for a few friends. This revolution is manifest not only in a lively curiosity about the practical techniques of foreign cuisines (Italian, Mexican, and especially French and Chinese) but in a loving, nostalgic glance at America's own past. Suddenly there is an eagerness to revive the plain good cooking that our mothers or grandmothers specialized in—the homemade breads, the fresh-churned butter, the cobblers and jellies and relishes that used to be in the repertory of every cook but that lately have been threatened by extinction. Perhaps the most encouraging development of all has been the return of the kitchen garden, planted and weeded by energetic souls who care about fresh herbs and berries and vegetables.

In no part of the country has this interest been keener than in the South. This is not surprising, for the Sunbelt is enjoying renewed prosperity, and in any case, Southerners have always loved to eat and drink well. More than other Americans, they have a well-defined tradition of cooking. It is not haute cuisine in every instance but there is a tradition too strong and stubborn to yield to the culinary trends working against regionalism. It may be the last surviving authentically regional mode of cooking left in America. For in the South, if nowhere else, there are many kitchens that let you know what neck of the woods you are in – delectably.

These kitchens are not always easy for the outsider to find. One of the best Southern lunches I ever had was served to me not long ago in, of all places, a motel dining room near Milledgeville, Georgia. It was nothing fancy, but the mustard greens, the cornbread, the fried chicken, and the berry cobbler were fresh and utterly delicious. When I expressed my delight to my hostess, Mrs. Regina O'Connor, mother of the late novelist Flannery O'Connor, she saw my poorly concealed astonishment, for she smiled rather wickedly, and replied, "Well, we have the good old cooks down here who know what we like and what we're used to."

Most good cooks, old or young, practice their art at home. Real Southern cuisine includes things that are indescribably delicious, as well as fattening. There is a house I know, down a dirt road in Garland County, Arkansas, where I eat so well, on the rare occasions I can manage to get there, that I wonder why I ever imagine I eat well anywhere else. That wonderful light, sour, white cornbread with fresh butter. Biscuits. Ham and maybe red-eye gravy. Pork chops and cream gravy, baked chicken and dressing. Okra rolled in cornmeal and fried. String beans cooked all day with fatmeat. Coconut cake and apple pie. All this is the work of my Aunt Frances, and it is the homeliest, plainest kind of Southern cooking. She only laughs when I tell her how good it is. She claims to have no idea how she does it. But in every good cook in America today there is something of an Aunt Frances, who can take a few fresh vegetables and a pan of biscuits and a slice of ham and turn them into a fine meal.

There is not likely to be any massive return, in the South or elsewhere, to this kind of cooking. It is too fattening, for one thing, and it is better adapted to wood stoves than to microwave ovens. Besides, in order for the table to be set with three platters of meat and six bowls of vegetables, which is about the proper number, a large family (preferably hungry from working in the fields all morning) is a necessity. And large families, as we all know, have long been out of style.

But the old traditions of Southern cooking will never die out entirely, and are clearly and deliciously reflected in a good number of the recipes in this book. A new cuisine has begun to evolve, less fundamentalist in its approach to eating and drinking, that takes full advantage of all kinds of new ingredients, methods, appliances, and tools. It is eclectic, borrowing readily from any promising source. It is literate – for Southern cooks, even those with a whole encyclopedia of family recipes in their heads, cook from cookbooks – without quite abandoning the "pinch of this" method. But, nevertheless, this new cuisine is homemade, devised by people who select the raw materials and transform them, as Proust's Françoise did.

Françoise was an artist. She did not know it and would not have accepted the designation, any more than my Aunt Frances would. "Art" always sounds like something remote, practiced anywhere but in the kitchen. And yet food and the fine arts are an ancient and honorable pair, and it is good cooks, fully as much as painters or architects, who create a civilization and are the measure of it. This book is, in its way, the testimonial of such cooks – for all the recipes are original, and come straight from the kitchens where they were created. The photographs, too, were especially made, bringing yet another kind of artistic eye to bear on the subject. Like the paintings in the book, the recipes are a combination of the present and the past. Perhaps the signs are right now, and an authentic new cooking style is about to emerge in America. If so, the movement will be directed by home cooks. And it will be a very civilized achievement.

Back-country Southern roads like this one, and back-country Southern cooking may soon be on the list of endangered species. But time-honored traditions will, in new forms, survive and continue. Photograph by Margaret MacKichan

Pieter Brueghel: The Harvesters, *1565, Metropolitan Museum of Art*

$\mathcal{B}$y $\mathcal{B}$read $\mathcal{A}$lone

$\mathcal{P}$ieter Brueghel's *The Harvesters,* opposite, is majestic in its sweep. We see men and women in a magnificent agricultural landscape, and the solidity of their bodies and faces perfectly matches their surroundings: they are at home. Some of them labor at the harvest, while others rest in the shade, having their dinner of porridge, fruit, and bread. Bread was the basis of the European peasant diet when this picture was painted, in 1565 — and long before and after. The people are part of the wheat fields as much as those fields are part of them. If one painting in all the world had to be taken as emblematic of human life, it could certainly be this one.

Bread has been the major staple of the diet of most people since the magic of leavening was discovered in Egypt, some six thousand years ago. The first yeast bread was probably a happy accident — the result of some micro-organism getting into a batch of dough at just the right moment and setting off the chemical process that causes bread to rise. The cook, one imagines, was probably tempted to throw the whole thing away, but then the end product turned out to be much more delicious than the usual flat-breads, and a culinary revolution took place. Ancient cooks tried various ferments — beer foam, wheat bran steeped in wine, wheat flour made into a kind of porridge and left to sour. The simplest method was to save a bit of dough each day and incorporate it into the next day's batch. In the past twenty years, the art of making bread at home has declined, but it has recently undergone a happy revival. The good cook can offer family and guests nothing more satisfying and impressive than a loaf of good, home-made bread.

The yeast breads photographed by Jerome Drown, and included in the recipes following, are whole wheat sourdough, New Orleans French, Sally Lunn, plaited white, and black.

17

Breads

The variety of Southern baking is best sampled from a board of homemade yeast breads. From Sally Lunn to New Orleans French bread, the flavors of home baking make for memories that are fresh long after the bread is gone.

Whole Wheat Sourdough Bread

1-1/2 cups boiling water
1/2 cup shortening
1 package dry yeast
1 teaspoon sugar
1 egg, well beaten
1/2 cup sugar
1/2 teaspoon salt
1 cup sourdough starter, at room temperature (recipe follows)
3 cups all-purpose flour, divided
2 cups whole wheat flour

Combine boiling water and shortening in a large bowl; allow to cool to 105° to 115°. Add yeast and 1 teaspoon sugar; let stand 15 minutes. Add egg, 1/2 cup sugar, salt, sourdough starter, and 2-1/2 cups all-purpose flour; beat at medium speed of electric mixer 3 minutes. Gradually stir in 1/2 cup all-purpose flour and whole wheat flour.

Turn dough out on a floured surface, and knead about 5 minutes or until smooth and elastic. Place dough in a greased bowl, turning to grease top. Cover with plastic wrap. Let rise in a warm place (85°), free from drafts, 1-1/2 to 2 hours or until dough is doubled in bulk.

Divide dough in half, and place on a floured surface. Roll each half into an 8- x 18-inch rectangle. Roll up, beginning at narrow edge; as you roll the dough, press firmly to eliminate air pockets. Pinch seams and ends together to seal. Place seam side down in 2 well-greased 9- x 5- x 3-inch loafpans.

Cover and let rise until doubled in bulk. Place in a cold oven. Bake at 400° for 15 minutes; reduce heat to 350°, and continue baking 20 minutes or until loaves sound hollow when tapped. Remove from pans; cool on wire racks. Yield: two 9- x 5-inch loaves.

Sourdough Starter:
1 package dry yeast
3 cups warm water (105° to 115°)
3-1/2 cups all-purpose flour

Combine yeast and water; set aside 5 minutes. Gradually add flour, beating at medium speed of electric mixer until smooth. Cover with plastic wrap. Place in a warm spot (85°), free from drafts, until bubbles appear on surface (about 24 hours). If starter has not started to ferment after 24 hours, discard it and start over.

Stir starter well; cover and return to warm place. Let stand 2 days or until foamy.

Stir well, and pour into an airtight glass container. Store in refrigerator. Stir before using, and allow to come to room temperature. Yield: about 4 cups.

Note: Starter may be stored in refrigerator several weeks, but it should be used weekly. If not used regularly, add 1 teaspoon sugar, stirring well. This will keep yeast active.

Onion-Dill Bread

2 packages dry yeast
1-1/4 cups warm water (105° to 115°)
1 egg, beaten
2 tablespoons sugar
3 tablespoons melted butter or margarine
1 teaspoon salt
1 medium onion, minced
2 teaspoons dill weed
1 cup lukewarm buttermilk
About 7-1/2 cups all-purpose flour

Dissolve yeast in warm water in a mixing bowl; add egg, sugar, butter, salt, onion, dill weed, and buttermilk, mixing well. Gradually add about half the flour; beat until smooth. Gradually add remaining flour to make a soft dough.

Turn dough out onto a lightly floured board; knead until smooth and elastic, about 7 minutes. Place dough in a greased bowl, turning to grease all sides. Cover and let rise in a warm place free from drafts until doubled in bulk, about 1 hour.

Punch dough down; turn onto a lightly floured board and knead lightly. Divide in half; shape each half into a loaf and place in 2 greased 9-1/4- x 5-1/4- x 2-3/4-inch loafpans. Cover; let rise in a warm place until doubled in bulk, about 1 hour. Bake at 350° for 35 to 45 minutes. Yield: 2 loaves.

Note: To make rolls, shape dough into 1-1/2-inch balls and place in 2 greased 9-inch round pans. Let rise until doubled in bulk, about 1 hour. Bake at 350° for 20 to 25 minutes. Yield: about 18 large rolls.

New Orleans French Bread

2 tablespoons shortening
1 tablespoon sugar
1 tablespoon salt
1 cup boiling water
1 cup cold water
1 package dry yeast
5-1/2 to 6 cups all-purpose flour, divided
Egg White Glaze

Combine shortening, sugar, salt, and boiling water in a large bowl; stir occasionally to melt shortening. Add cold water, and allow mixture to cool to 105° to 115°. Sprinkle yeast over liquid mixture; let stand 5 minutes, and stir to dissolve. Gradually beat in 4 cups flour; add enough remaining flour to form a stiff dough.

Turn dough out onto a floured surface, and knead until smooth and elastic (about 5 minutes). Place in a well-greased bowl, turning once to grease top. Cover with a damp cloth. Let rise in a warm place (85°), free from drafts, 1 to 1-1/2 hours or until doubled in bulk. Punch down; cover. Let rise 30 minutes or until doubled in bulk.

Turn dough onto a floured surface; knead slightly to press out gas bubbles; shape into a 14- to 16-inch cylinder on a greased baking sheet. Cover; let rise until doubled in bulk.

Cut 1/4-inch-deep slashes in top of loaf with a sharp knife; brush with Egg White Glaze. Bake at 375° for 40 to 50 minutes or until golden brown. Remove from baking sheet; cool on wire rack. Yield: 1 loaf.

Egg White Glaze:
1 egg white
2 tablespoons cold water

Combine egg white and water, beating until frothy. Yield: glaze for 1 loaf.

Detail of Scene from the Life of St. Nicholas of Bari *by Fra Angelico, shows two men bagging grain. Vatican Museum*

Plaited White Bread

1 package dry yeast
2 cups warm water (105° to 115°)
1/3 cup sugar
2 teaspoons salt
1 egg, well beaten
6 to 7 cups all-purpose flour, divided
3 tablespoons salad oil

Combine yeast, warm water, sugar, salt, and egg in a large bowl; set aside 5 minutes. Gradually add 3 cups flour, beating well. Add salad oil and 3 to 4 cups flour to form a stiff dough.

Turn dough out on a floured surface, and knead until smooth and elastic (5 to 8 minutes). Place in a well-greased bowl, turning to grease top. Cover with plastic wrap. Let rise in a warm place (85°), free from drafts, 1-1/2 to 2 hours or until doubled in bulk.

Punch dough down, and divide into thirds. Shape each third into a 14- to 16-inch rope. Place ropes on a greased baking sheet, and firmly pinch ends together at one end to seal. Braid ropes together, and pinch loose ends to seal.

Cover; let rise in a warm place, free from drafts, until doubled in bulk. Bake at 350° for 20 to 25 minutes or until lightly browned. Yield: 1 loaf.

Sally Lunn

1 package dry yeast
1/4 cup warm water (105° to 115°)
3/4 cup warm milk
1/2 cup butter or margarine, softened
1/3 cup sugar
3 eggs, well beaten
4 cups all-purpose flour
1 teaspoon salt

Combine yeast and water in a small bowl; let stand 5 minutes. Stir in milk. Cream butter and sugar until light and fluffy in a large bowl; add eggs, blending well.

Combine flour and salt; add to creamed mixture alternately with milk mixture, beginning and ending with flour. Mix well after each addition. (Batter will be very stiff.) Cover with plastic wrap. Let rise in a warm place (85°), free from drafts, about 2 hours or until doubled in bulk.

Spoon batter into a well-greased 10-inch tube pan or Bundt pan. Cover with plastic wrap. Let rise in a warm place, free from drafts, until doubled in bulk. Bake at 350° for 50 to 60 minutes. Remove from pan; cool on wire rack. Yield: one 10-inch loaf.

Monkey Bread

1 cup milk
1 cup butter or margarine, melted and divided
4 tablespoons sugar
1 teaspoon salt
1 package dry yeast
3-1/2 cups all-purpose flour

Combine milk, 1/2 cup butter, sugar, and salt in a saucepan; heat until butter is melted. Cool to 105° to 115°; stir in yeast until dissolved. Place flour in a large bowl; make a well in flour and pour in liquid mixture. Stir until blended.

Cover and let rise until doubled in bulk, about 1 hour and 20 minutes. Turn dough out on a floured surface. Roll 1/4 inch thick. Cut into 3-inch squares. Dip each square into remaining butter.

Layer squares in a 10-inch tube or Bundt pan. Let rise until doubled in bulk, about 30 to 40 minutes. Bake at 375° for 30 to 40 minutes. Yield: about 6 servings.

Bran Rolls

1 cup boiling water
1 cup shredded wheat bran cereal
3/4 cup shortening
3/4 cup sugar
1 package dry yeast
1 cup warm water (105° to 115°)
1-1/4 teaspoons salt
2 eggs, beaten
About 6 cups all-purpose flour

Combine boiling water, cereal, shortening, and sugar; set aside. Dissolve yeast in warm water; add salt and eggs. Combine cereal mixture and yeast mixture in a large mixing bowl. Stir in enough flour to make a soft dough.

Place dough in a greased bowl, turning to grease all sides; cover and refrigerate overnight.

Punch dough down, and turn out on a lightly floured board; knead lightly. Roll dough into 1-1/2-inch balls, and place in 2 greased 9-inch pans and 1 greased 8-inch pan. Cover; let rise in a warm place until doubled in bulk (about 2 hours). Bake at 375° for 10 to 12 minutes or until browned. Yield: about 4 dozen.

Note: Dough may be made into rolls without refrigerating overnight. Turn out onto a lightly floured board; knead lightly. Shape as directed; cover and let rise in a warm place about 1 hour. Bake as directed.

Detail from July Hay, *a painting done in 1943 by Thomas Hart Benton, a native of Missouri.* MMA

Black Bread

1 package dry yeast
2 cups warm water (105° to 115°)
2 tablespoons sugar
2 teaspoons salt
2 tablespoons shortening, melted and cooled
4 to 5 cups all-purpose flour, divided
3 tablespoons dark molasses
3 cups rye flour
1 tablespoon caraway seeds
1 tablespoon dillseeds
Melted butter or margarine

Dissolve yeast in warm water in a large bowl. Add sugar, salt, shortening, and 3 cups all-purpose flour; beat well. Add molasses, rye flour, caraway seeds, and dillseeds. Stir in enough additional all-purpose flour to form a stiff dough.

Turn dough out on a floured surface, and knead until smooth and elastic (about 8 to 10 minutes). Place in a well-greased bowl, turning to grease top. Cover with plastic wrap or a towel. Let rise in a warm place (85°), free from drafts, until doubled in bulk.

Divide dough in half, and shape each half into a smooth ball. Place each on a greased baking sheet, and lightly press to flatten bottom. Cover; let rise in a warm place, free from drafts, until doubled in bulk. Bake at 400° for 30 minutes or until loaves sound hollow when tapped. Brush hot loaves with melted butter. Remove from baking sheets; cool on wire racks. Yield: 2 loaves.

Pierre Bonnard:
The Breakfast Room,
1930-31,
Museum of Modern Art

Breaking the Fast

A palpable sense of domestic tranquillity pervades the scene opposite: a summer morning with a window open on a garden, a table set for breakfast. Pierre Bonnard was over sixty when he painted this picture, but he was at the peak of his artistic powers. (He continued to work steadily and productively until the day of his death in 1947, at the age of 79.) He never seriously tried to do anything but paint, and he cared nothing for money or the glamorous bohemian life. He painted what he loved and understood. According to the testimony of his friend Paul Signac, the Fauvist painter, Bonnard loved and understood everything—"the pie for dessert, the eye of his dog, a ray of sunshine coming through his window blind, the sponge in his bathtub." Like his contemporary Cézanne, he chose for his subjects the most commonplace household objects and, by some alchemy of color and light, transfigured them. He loved the same woman all his life and lived serenely with her for thirty years before they took the trouble to get married. They lived in a small house in the South of France, and though they had many friends, they clung to their privacy. It is said that when Bonnard spotted a stranger approaching, he would go out to the front gate and announce, "Monsieur Bonnard is not at home." What he wanted most, he once said, was "to paint the savor of things." And in the scene opposite, he has surely caught the savor of a leisurely morning with a well-set table beside an open window. The brioches at right and the recipes that follow will also ensure domestic tranquillity, when there is time to spend an hour or two on the first meal of the day.

Brioches photographed by Taylor Lewis

Breakfast

The warm aroma of good work being done in a morning kitchen rouses the slugabed and makes the early riser impatient.

Apricot-Nut Bread

2-1/2 cups all-purpose flour
1 cup sugar
3-1/2 teaspoons baking powder
1 tablespoon plus 1 teaspoon grated
  orange peel
3 tablespoons vegetable oil
1/2 cup milk
3/4 cup orange juice
1 egg, slightly beaten
1 cup finely chopped pecans
1 cup finely cut dried apricots

Combine all ingredients in a large bowl; mix until well blended. Pour into a greased and floured 9- x 5- x 3-inch loafpan. Bake at 350° for 55 to 65 minutes. Cool 10 minutes in pan; remove from pan. Yield: 1 loaf.

Butter Muffins

2 cups muffin mix (recipe follows)
1 tablespoon sugar
1 egg, slightly beaten
3/4 cup milk

Combine muffin mix, sugar, egg, and milk. Stir just to moisten. Fill well-greased muffin pans two-thirds full. Bake at 425° for 20 to 25 minutes or until lightly browned. Yield: 1 dozen.

Muffin Mix:
5-1/2 cups all-purpose flour
4 tablespoons baking powder
1/2 cup sugar
1-1/2 teaspoons salt
1/2 cup butter or margarine, softened

Combine flour, baking powder, sugar, and salt; cut in butter until mixture resembles cornmeal. Store, tightly covered, in refrigerator until ready to use. Yield: about 6 cups.

Brioche

1/2 cup milk
1/2 cup softened margarine
1/3 cup sugar
1 teaspoon salt
1 package dry yeast
1/4 cup warm water (105° to 115°)
3 eggs
1 egg yolk
3-1/2 cups all-purpose flour
1 egg white
1 tablespoon sugar

Scald milk; cool to lukewarm. Combine margarine, 1/3 cup sugar, and salt in a large mixing bowl; cream until light and fluffy.

Sprinkle yeast into warm water; stir until dissolved. Add yeast mixture, milk, eggs, egg yolk, and flour to creamed mixture. Beat vigorously 2 minutes with a wooden spoon. Cover and let rise in a warm place free from drafts until more than doubled in bulk (about 2 hours). Punch dough down; beat vigorously 2 minutes. Cover tightly with aluminum foil, and refrigerate overnight.

Beat dough down, and turn out onto a lightly floured board. Divide into 2 portions, one about three-fourths of dough and the other about one-fourth of dough.

Cut larger portion of dough into 24 equal pieces, and form each into a smooth ball. Place in well-greased muffin pans. Cut smaller portion of dough into 24 equal pieces, and form each into a smooth ball.

Make a deep indentation in center of each large ball; dampen slightly with cold water. Press a small ball into each indentation. Let rise in a warm place free from drafts about 50 minutes or until doubled in bulk.

Combine egg white and 1 tablespoon sugar; brush each brioche with egg white mixture. Bake at 375° about 15 to 20 minutes. Yield: 2 dozen.

Sour Cream Waffles

1 cup all-purpose flour
1-1/2 teaspoons sugar
1/4 teaspoon salt
1/4 teaspoon soda
1 egg, separated
1 cup commercial sour cream

Combine flour, sugar, salt, and soda. Stir in egg yolk and sour cream, mixing lightly.

Beat egg white until stiff; fold into batter. Bake in preheated waffle iron. Yield: 4 waffles.

French Waffle Toast

6 eggs, beaten
1 cup half-and-half
1/4 cup melted butter or margarine
Pinch of salt and pepper
3 drops Worcestershire sauce
3 drops hot sauce
2 tablespoons sugar
1/2 cup maple-flavored syrup
Pinch of ground cinnamon
1/2 teaspoon ground nutmeg
1 (16-ounce) loaf French bread, sliced thick

Combine all ingredients except bread in a large mixing bowl; beat well about 2 minutes. Dip slices of bread one at a time in the batter, coating well. Let drain; place on waffle iron preheated to 375°. Cook about 2 minutes or until brown.

Leftover batter can be stored in refrigerator 10 days. Yield: 10 to 12 servings.

Apple Butter Bread

2 cups self-rising flour
1/4 cup sugar
1-1/2 teaspoons ground cinnamon
2 eggs, beaten
3/4 cup apple butter
1/4 cup melted butter or margarine
2 tablespoons apple juice
1/2 cup chopped nuts
1/2 cup raisins

Combine flour, sugar, and cinnamon; set aside. Combine eggs, apple butter, butter, and apple juice; add to flour mixture, blending well. Stir in nuts and raisins. Pour into a greased 8-1/2- x 4-1/2-inch loafpan. Bake at 350° for 55 minutes. Cool 10 minutes before removing from pan. Yield: 1 loaf.

Baked Pancake with Apple Syrup

2 tablespoons butter or margarine
2/3 cup all-purpose flour
2/3 cup milk
1/2 teaspoon baking powder
4 eggs, beaten
Apple Syrup

Melt butter in an ovenproof 12-inch skillet at 400°. Combine flour, milk, baking powder, and eggs; mix well. Pour batter into hot skillet. Bake 15 to 18 minutes or until puffy and golden. Cut into wedges; serve hot with Apple Syrup. Yield: 6 to 8 servings.

Apple Syrup:

**2 medium cooking apples, peeled and
thinly sliced**
1/2 cup maple syrup

Combine apples and maple syrup in a small saucepan. Bring to a boil; reduce heat and simmer 2 minutes or until the apples are tender. Yield: about 1-2/3 cups.

Refrigerator Bran Muffins

**1 (15-ounce) box wheat bran flakes cereal
with raisins**
5 cups all-purpose flour
3 cups sugar
5 teaspoons soda
2 teaspoons salt
4 eggs, beaten
1 quart buttermilk
1 cup shortening, melted

Combine first 5 ingredients in a large bowl; make a well in center of mixture. Add eggs, buttermilk, and shortening; stir just enough to moisten dry ingredients. Cover and store in refrigerator until ready to bake, as long as five to six weeks.

When ready to bake, spoon batter into greased muffin tins, filling two-thirds full. Bake at 350° for 20 minutes. Yield: about 5-1/2 dozen.

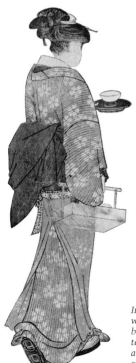

*In the Orient, tea is taken
with every meal, including
breakfast. At left, a Japanese
teahouse waitress. Detail from
a print by Utamaro. Museum
of Fine Arts, Boston*

Rolled French Pancakes

1/2 cup all-purpose flour
1/8 teaspoon salt
1 egg, beaten
1 egg yolk, beaten
1/2 cup milk
Vegetable oil
3 tablespoons jelly
Powdered sugar

Combine flour, salt, egg, egg yolk, and milk; beat until smooth. Cover and chill 30 minutes.

Brush a 5-inch skillet lightly with vegetable oil; place over medium heat until just hot, not smoking. Pour 2 tablespoons batter in skillet; quickly tilt in all directions so batter covers the bottom in a thin film. Cook about 1 minute; lift edge of pancake to test for doneness. Turn pancake, and cook about 30 seconds on other side.

Spread each pancake with jelly; roll up jelly-roll fashion. Place on baking sheet, and sprinkle with powdered sugar. Place under broiler just until glazed. Yield: about 8 pancakes.

Orange Waffles

3 cups all-purpose flour
2 tablespoons baking powder
2 teaspoons sugar
1 teaspoon salt
6 eggs, separated
1-1/2 cups half-and-half
4 teaspoons grated orange rind
1 cup orange juice
1/2 cup melted butter or margarine
Orange-Currant Syrup

Combine flour, baking powder, sugar, and salt in a large bowl; set aside. Beat egg yolks until lemon colored; stir in half-and-half, orange rind, orange juice, and butter. Add to dry ingredients, mixing well.

Beat egg whites until stiff peaks form; fold into batter. Bake in hot waffle iron until done. Serve with Orange-Currant Syrup. Yield: about six 10-inch waffles.

Orange-Currant Syrup:
1 tablespoon cornstarch
1/2 cup orange juice
1/2 cup currant jelly

Combine cornstarch and orange juice in a small saucepan, mixing well. Add jelly. Cook over medium heat until thickened, stirring constantly. Serve hot. Yield: about 1 cup.

English Muffins

1 cup milk
3 tablespoons shortening
1-1/2 teaspoons salt
3 tablespoons sugar
1 package dry yeast
1/4 cup warm water (105° to 115°)
1 egg, beaten
4-1/4 cups all-purpose flour, divided
Melted shortening

Scald milk, and stir in shortening, salt, and sugar; cool to lukewarm. Sprinkle yeast into warm water; stir well, and add to milk mixture. Add egg and 2 cups flour, mixing well.

Turn dough out on a lightly floured board; knead in remaining flour until smooth and elastic. Place in a large greased bowl, and brush with melted shortening; cover and let rise in a warm place about 1-1/2 hours.

Turn dough out on a lightly floured board, and roll to 1/4-inch thickness. Cut with a 3-1/2-inch round cutter, and place on an ungreased baking sheet. Let rise in a warm place about 45 minutes or until doubled in bulk. Bake at 325° about 8 minutes on one side; turn muffins, and bake about 8 minutes on other side. Yield: about 1 dozen.

Funnel Cakes

1-1/4 cups all-purpose flour
2 tablespoons sugar
1 teaspoon soda
3/4 teaspoon baking powder
1/4 teaspoon salt
1 egg
3/4 cup milk
Vegetable oil
2 teaspoons powdered sugar
Syrup

Combine dry ingredients; add egg and milk, beating until smooth.

Heat 1 inch oil to 375° in a deep skillet. Cover bottom opening of a funnel with finger. Pour 1/4 cup batter into funnel. Hold funnel over center of skillet. Remove finger from funnel end to release batter into hot oil; move funnel in a slow circular motion to form a spiral, beginning at the center and moving outward.

Fry 2 minutes or until golden brown, turning once. Drain on paper towels. Sprinkle with powdered sugar; serve hot with syrup. Yield: 6 servings.

George C. Bingham: Shooting for the Beef, *1850, The Brooklyn Museum*

Prime and Choice

George Caleb Bingham was, as he wanted to be, a social historian. As a painter of American frontier life, mainly in the river towns of Missouri, he saw his task as capturing "our social and political characteristics." In 1850, he made one of his finest genre paintings, *Shooting for the Beef,* opposite, which shows not only what American frontiersmen enjoyed as sport but also how highly they prized one food above all. A group of men, well fed and happy, compete in a shooting match. The prize is a steer, with the winner getting the valuable "fifth quarter"—hide and tallow—and the other sharpshooters the rest. Such contests were not rare in mid-nineteenth-century Missouri. "Many of the most distinguished guns acquire names of the most fearful import," wrote a columnist in a Boone's Lick, Missouri, newspaper in 1825, "and small bets are sometimes made on Black Snake, Cross Burster, Hair Splitter, Blood Letter, and Panther Cooler."

In the century following the American Revolution, pork was America's most popular meat—or at least the most widely available, particularly in the Southern states. But with the advent of a nationwide cattle industry, late in the nineteenth century, beef quickly replaced it. Beef Wellington, right, is one of the loftier permutations of the roast. It may by now have replaced even the turkey as the hallmark of a grand occasion.

Beef Wellington photographed by Kent Kirkley

Beef

Among entrées, beef is the American favorite. From the modest hamburger to an estimable filet mignon, all are very much at home on the range.

Standing Rib Roast

1 (6-1/2-pound) standing rib roast
Salt and pepper to taste
12 large mushrooms
About 2 tablespoons vegetable oil
1/4 cup sliced green onion
3 tablespoons melted butter or margarine
1/3 cup breadcrumbs
1/2 teaspoon dried dillweed
1/4 teaspoon salt
Dash of Worcestershire sauce
Parsley (optional)
Cherry tomatoes (optional)

Sprinkle roast with salt and pepper. Place roast, fat side up, on rack in a shallow roasting pan. Insert meat thermometer, making certain end of thermometer does not touch fat or bone.

Bake at 325° as follows, depending on desired degree of doneness: rare, 27 minutes per pound or 140° on meat thermometer; medium, 30 minutes per pound or 160°; well done, 36 minutes per pound or 170°.

Let roast stand at room temperature about 15 minutes before carving.

Trim mushroom stems. Gently rinse mushrooms, and pat dry. Remove and chop stems. Brush outside of caps with vegetable oil, and place in a buttered baking dish.

Sauté chopped mushrooms and onion in butter until tender; stir in breadcrumbs, dillweed, 1/4 teaspoon salt, and Worcestershire. Stuff mushroom caps with breadcrumb mixture. Bake at 325° for 15 minutes; arrange around roast. Garnish roast with parsley and cherry tomatoes, if desired. Yield: 12 servings.

Beef Wellington

Pastry (recipe follows)
1 (5- to 5-1/2-pound) beef tenderloin
2 (4-3/4-ounce) cans liver pâté
1 egg, beaten
1 teaspoon cold water

Prepare pastry; chill at least 1 hour.

Trim fat from tenderloin; reserve. Tuck small end of meat underneath tenderloin; tie securely with string at 2-inch intervals. Place meat on rack in an open pan. Lay pieces of fat on top of meat. (Do not add water, and do not cover.) Roast at 425° for 20 to 25 minutes for rare; 25 to 30 minutes for medium.

Remove meat from oven, and discard fat. Let stand 30 minutes to cool. Remove string; keep small end of meat tucked underneath.

Roll pastry into an 18- x 14-inch rectangle on a lightly floured board or pastry cloth. Spread pâté over pastry to within 1 inch of edge.

Place tenderloin lengthwise, top side down, in middle of pastry. Bring long sides of pastry up to overlap on underside of tenderloin. Combine egg and water; brush seam with egg mixture to seal. Trim ends of pastry and fold over; brush with egg mixture to seal.

Place meat, seam side down, on a lightly greased baking sheet. Brush with egg mixture.

Roll pastry trimmings; cut into decorative shapes and arrange on top of tenderloin. Brush with remaining egg mixture. Bake at 425° for 30 minutes or until pastry is golden. Let stand 10 minutes before slicing. Garnish as desired. Yield: 12 to 14 servings.

Pastry:
3 cups all-purpose flour
1/2 teaspoon salt
3/4 cup shortening
1/2 to 3/4 cup cold water

Combine flour and salt; cut in shortening with pastry blender until mixture resembles coarse cornmeal. Add water, 1 tablespoon at a time, stirring with a fork until dough holds together. Shape into a ball. Wrap in waxed paper and chill until ready to use.

Decorated roast, from a 19th-century book, Artistic Cookery

Steak Diane Flambé

2 cups sliced fresh mushrooms or
   2 (4-ounce) cans sliced mushrooms, drained
1/4 cup finely chopped shallots
2/3 to 3/4 cup melted butter or
   margarine, divided
1 teaspoon chopped chives
2 teaspoons chopped parsley
1/2 teaspoon Worcestershire sauce
1/2 teaspoon salt
2 teaspoons freshly ground pepper
2 (8-ounce) filets mignons, halved crosswise
1/3 cup cognac
3 tablespoons dry sherry

Sauté mushrooms and shallots in 1/2 cup butter in a small saucepan 5 minutes. Add seasonings, and simmer 15 minutes. Set aside.

Sauté filets in the remaining melted butter until desired degree of doneness. Heat cognac over medium heat; do not boil. Ignite and pour over filets. When flame is extinguished, add sherry. Transfer filets to a heated platter; spoon mushroom mixture over filets. Serve immediately. Yield: 2 to 4 servings.

Pot Roast with Vegetables

1 (4-pound) rump roast
2 tablespoons all-purpose flour
1 tablespoon salt
1/4 teaspoon pepper
2 tablespoons hot vegetable oil
1 cup water
1/2 to 1 teaspoon thick, spicy steak sauce
6 carrots, cut in 2-inch pieces
4 large potatoes, peeled and quartered
1 large onion, peeled and cut in 1/2-inch slices
Salt and pepper

Wipe roast with a damp paper towel. Combine flour, 1 tablespoon salt, and 1/4 teaspoon pepper; rub into roast. Brown roast on all sides in oil in a Dutch oven.

Remove pan from heat; stir in water and steak sauce. Cover tightly and cook over low heat 1 hour and 15 minutes.

Add vegetables to meat, and sprinkle with salt and pepper to taste. Cover and cook over low heat 45 minutes or until meat and vegetables are tender. Yield: 8 servings.

Tenderloin Tips in Wine

6 tablespoons butter or margarine, divided
1 pound beef tenderloin, cut into strips
  1/4 inch wide
2 medium onions, chopped
2 medium-size green peppers, chopped
1-1/2 teaspoons salt
1/2 to 1 teaspoon pepper
1 (10-1/4-ounce) can brown gravy
1 cup Burgundy or other dry red wine
2 tablespoons cornstarch
Hot cooked rice

Melt 2 tablespoons butter in a large skillet; add tenderloin, and sauté until brown. Remove meat, and set aside.

Melt 4 tablespoons butter in skillet; add onion, green pepper, salt, and pepper. Sauté 3 minutes; stir in gravy.

Combine Burgundy and cornstarch, mixing well; pour into skillet. Cook on medium heat until bubbly, stirring constantly. Cook on low heat 2 minutes, stirring occasionally. Add meat, stirring well. Serve over rice. Yield: 4 servings.

Chinese Pepper Steak

1 (1-pound) boneless chuck roast, cut into
  1-inch strips
1 teaspoon salt
1/4 cup vegetable oil
2 tablespoons soy sauce
1 clove garlic, minced
1-1/2 cups water, divided
1 cup green pepper strips
1 large onion, sliced
1/2 cup sliced celery
2 tomatoes, cut into wedges
1 tablespoon cornstarch
Hot cooked rice

Sprinkle meat with salt; brown quickly in hot oil. Add soy sauce, garlic, and 1/2 cup water; bring to a boil. Cover and simmer over low heat 45 minutes or until tender. Add green pepper, onion, and celery. Cover and simmer 10 minutes. Add tomatoes; toss lightly.

Combine cornstarch and 1 cup water; stir until cornstarch is dissolved. Add to meat mixture; cook over medium heat, stirring constantly, until mixture boils. Boil 1 minute or until slightly thickened. Serve over rice. Yield: 4 to 6 servings.

Tenderloin of Beef

1 (6- to 7-pound) beef tenderloin, trimmed
Garlic salt to taste
Salt and pepper to taste

Rub tenderloin with seasonings; place fat side up on rack in a shallow roasting pan. Bake at 450° for 15 minutes. Turn oven off; do not open door. Let roast remain in oven 45 minutes. Roast will be medium rare. Yield: 8 to 10 servings.

Gold Crowned Meat Loaf

1-1/2 cups soft breadcrumbs
1-1/2 pounds ground beef
4 eggs, separated
1-1/2 teaspoons salt
2 tablespoons minced onion
1/2 cup catsup
6 tablespoons prepared mustard, divided
1-1/2 teaspoons prepared horseradish
3 tablespoons finely chopped green pepper
1/4 teaspoon cream of tartar

Combine breadcrumbs and beef; set aside. Combine egg yolks, salt, onion, catsup, 2 tablespoons mustard, horseradish, and green pepper; blend into meat mixture. Lightly pack into a 9-inch baking dish. Bake at 325° for 30 minutes.

Beat egg whites until foamy. Add cream of tartar, and beat until very stiff. Gently fold in remaining 4 tablespoons mustard. Spoon over meat loaf. Bake 20 to 25 minutes or until lightly browned. Yield: 6 to 8 servings.

Crabmeat-Stuffed Steak

1/2 cup chopped onion
1 clove garlic, minced
2 tablespoons melted butter or margarine
1 (4-ounce) can sliced mushrooms, drained
1/2 pound fresh or frozen crabmeat
1 tablespoon Worcestershire sauce
1 porterhouse or sirloin steak, cut 1-1/2
  inches thick

Sauté onion and garlic in butter until onion is tender. Add mushrooms, crabmeat, and Worcestershire sauce; mix well, and set aside.

Trim excess fat from steak. Cut a deep pocket into side of steak. Stuff pocket with crabmeat mixture; seal with skewers or toothpicks.

Broil steak 3 to 4 inches from heat for 5 to 6 minutes on each side or until desired doneness. Yield: 4 servings.

Herbed Rib Roast

1 tablespoon vegetable oil
1 (3-rib) standing rib roast
2 teaspoons oregano
2 teaspoons salt
1 teaspoon pepper
1 teaspoon paprika
1 teaspoon garlic powder

Rub oil over surface of roast. Combine remaining ingredients, and rub over roast. Place roast, fat side up, in a shallow baking pan. Insert meat thermometer, making certain end of thermometer does not touch fat or bone.

Bake at 350° as follows, depending on desired degree of doneness: 20 minutes per pound for rare or 140° on meat thermometer; medium, 25 to 30 minutes per pound or 160°; well done, 30 to 35 minutes per pound or 170°.

Let roast stand at room temperature about 15 minutes before carving. Yield: 6 servings.

German-Style Meatballs

1-1/2 pounds ground beef
2 eggs, beaten
2 tablespoons breadcrumbs
2 tablespoons instant minced onion
2 tablespoons parsley flakes
1-1/2 teaspoons salt
1/4 teaspoon pepper
1 tablespoon lemon juice
3 tablespoons beef broth granules
3 cups boiling water
3 tablespoons all-purpose flour
1/4 cup cold water
1 tablespoon Worcestershire sauce
3 tablespoons hamburger relish
Hot cooked noodles

Combine first 8 ingredients; shape into 2-inch balls.

Combine beef broth granules and boiling water. Add meatballs; heat to boiling. Lower heat; turn meatballs. Cover and simmer 30 minutes. Remove meatballs, and keep warm. Skim fat from broth; keep broth simmering.

Combine flour and cold water; gradually stir into broth. Add Worcestershire sauce and hamburger relish. Cook over medium heat, stirring constantly, until sauce thickens and bubbles. Pour sauce over meatballs. Serve over noodles. Yield: 4 to 6 servings.

Duccio di Buoninsegna: The Calling of the Apostles Peter and Andrew, *1308-11, National Gallery of Art, Washington, D.C.*

Net Results

Bream in beer batter photographed by Jerome Drown

Generally speaking, Americans and Europeans are carnivorous bipeds —that is, they have a long-standing and outspoken preference for meat. They look upon fish as possibly more interesting than a vegetable but certainly less so than a steak. Yet fish has always figured importantly in our diet, and the lore of fish is very rich. Fish was for centuries regarded as an aphrodisiac. A seventeenth-century Frenchman, Nicholas Venette, was of the opinion that his countrymen "feel most amorously inclined during Lent." More recently, fish has been touted as "brain food," and this may turn out to have some merit. A group of scientists studying brain chemistry have discovered that fish contains large amounts of a substance called choline, which under certain circumstances seems to improve the memory. Whether science will validate the link between fish and love remains to be seen, but, meanwhile, fresh fish on a platter, as shown at right, hardly needs to serve any higher purpose.

Fish, more than any other food, is connected with Christianity. The first Christians took the fish as their symbol—naturally enough, since Jesus had promised to make his followers fishers of men. In the painted panel opposite, an early work of the Italian Renaissance, Christ recruits his two seafaring disciples, Simon Peter and Andrew. The artist, Duccio di Buoninsegna, was a Siennese master of the late thirteenth and early fourteenth centuries. Here he has used the traditional gold background of the medieval artist, but he has added a touch of freshly observed life—fish darting through the water and being caught in a net. The panel was part of an altarpiece painted for the Siena Cathedral between 1308 and 1311. It was carried to the cathedral, it is said, amid great public rejoicing—"All the shops were shut, and the bishop led a great and devout company of priests and dignitaries in solemn procession . . . all the bells ringing joyfully."

Fish

"There are lots of good fish in the sea," sings the chorus to close Gilbert and Sullivan's <u>Mikado</u>. And many more of them in our fresh-water streams, rivers, and lakes. All rules of fish cookery are subsidiary to James Beard's unnumbered commandment: "Thou shalt not overcook."

Crisp Fried Catfish

6 small catfish, cleaned and dressed
1 teaspoon salt
1/4 teaspoon pepper
1 (2-ounce) bottle hot sauce
2 cups self-rising cornmeal
Salad oil

Sprinkle catfish with salt and pepper. Marinate in hot sauce for 1 to 2 hours in refrigerator.

Place cornmeal in a paper bag; drop in catfish one at a time, and shake until coated completely. Fry in deep hot oil over high heat until fish float to the top and are golden brown. Drain well. Serve hot. Yield: 4 to 6 servings.

Steamed Fish Fillets

1-1/2 pounds fish fillets
Soy sauce to taste
1/2 to 3/4 cup sliced green onions
1/2 cup very hot peanut oil
Lemon juice (optional)

Place fish on a rack above boiling water; cover and steam 2 to 3 minutes on each side or until fish turns white. Place fillets in a heatproof serving dish; sprinkle with soy sauce and onion. Pour hot oil over fish. When sizzling stops, serve immediately. Sprinkle with lemon juice, if desired. Yield: 4 servings.

Note: Get everything ready for this dish before starting, as it only takes about 5 minutes to prepare.

Crab-Stuffed Flounder

4 (1-1/2-pound) flounder or 1 (6- to 8-pound) flounder
1/3 cup minced onion
1/3 cup minced green pepper
1 cup melted butter
1-1/2 pounds crabmeat
Salt and pepper to taste
1/4 cup chopped parsley
2 tablespoons lemon juice
Dash of hot sauce
Additional melted butter
Additional lemon juice
Parsley
Notched lemon halves
Paprika
Seafood sauce (recipe follows)

Lay each fish flat on a cutting board, light side down; slit lengthwise, beginning 3/4 inch from head and cutting down center of fish to tail. Make a crosswise slit in flounder near head. Cut flesh along both sides of backbone to the tail, allowing the knife to run over the rib bones to form a pocket for stuffing.

Sauté onion and green pepper in 1 cup melted butter in a large skillet over medium heat; cook until onion is transparent. Remove from heat. Add crabmeat, salt, pepper, chopped parsley, 2 tablespoons lemon juice, and hot sauce; mix thoroughly.

Brush pocket of fish with melted butter, and sprinkle with salt and pepper. Stuff fish loosely with crabmeat mixture, and place on a greased baking sheet. Bake at 350° for 40 to 60 minutes (depending on size of fish) or until fish flakes easily when tested with a fork; baste frequently with additional butter and lemon juice as fish bakes.

Remove fish to serving platter, and garnish with parsley and notched lemon halves dipped in paprika. Top with seafood sauce before serving. Yield: 8 to 10 servings.

Seafood Sauce:

6 tablespoons melted butter
6 tablespoons all-purpose flour
Fish stock (recipe follows)
Salt and pepper to taste
1/3 cup chopped shrimp
1/3 cup crabmeat

Combine butter and flour in a saucepan, blending until smooth. Place over medium heat; cook, stirring constantly, 2 to 3 minutes or until frothy. Heat 3 cups fish stock to boiling, and gradually add to flour mixture; cook until thickened, stirring constantly. Add remaining ingredients, and simmer 5 minutes. Yield: about 3 cups.

Fish Stock:

2 pounds fish trimmings (heads, bones, or skin)
About 4 cups water
1/3 cup sliced carrot
1/3 cup sliced onion
1/3 cup sliced celery
1 bay leaf
1/2 teaspoon dried parsley
1/4 teaspoon salt
1/8 teaspoon pepper

Combine all ingredients in a saucepan. Simmer, uncovered, 30 minutes; let liquid cook down to about 3-1/2 cups. Strain stock, discarding residue; cool and skim off fat. Cover and refrigerate. If stock will not be used immediately, store in freezer; keeps well several weeks. Yield: about 3 cups.

A Coptic relief from the Louvre, Paris

Beer Batter Bream

6 to 8 bream, cleaned and dressed
Lemon juice
2 cups all-purpose flour, divided
Salt
1 tablespoon paprika
1 (12-ounce) can beer
Vegetable oil
Watercress or parsley sprigs
Lemon wedges

Dry fish thoroughly, and sprinkle lemon juice over both sides; let stand 15 minutes.

Combine 1 cup flour and 1 teaspoon salt; set aside.

Combine 1 cup flour, paprika, and 1 tablespoon salt; add beer, stirring until well blended.

Dredge fish in flour mixture; dip into beer batter. Fry fish until golden brown on both sides in 1/2 inch oil heated to 370°. Drain on paper towels. Garnish with watercress and lemon wedges. Yield: 6 to 8 servings.

Note: Batter may be stored in refrigerator 3 to 4 days.

Special Fried Fish

2 pounds fish fillets
1 teaspoon salt
Pepper
2 eggs, beaten
1/4 cup water
1/2 teaspoon prepared mustard
1/4 teaspoon onion powder
2-1/2 cups cracker crumbs
1/2 cup melted butter or margarine

Dry fish thoroughly, and cut into serving-size portions. Sprinkle both sides with salt and pepper. Combine eggs, water, mustard, and onion powder.

Dip both sides of fish into egg mixture, and coat with cracker crumbs; repeat process.

Fry fish in melted butter over low heat until golden brown on both sides. Drain on paper towels. Yield: about 6 servings.

Broiled Grouper Fillets

4 (4-ounce) grouper fillets
Juice of 1/2 lime
Freshly ground pepper
1 medium onion, thinly sliced
4 slices bacon
Mayonnaise

Arrange fillets in a shallow pan; sprinkle with lime juice and pepper. Cover fish with onion slices, and place bacon slices on top.

Broil 3 inches from source of heat about 5 minutes; remove from oven and brush lightly with mayonnaise. Broil 2 to 3 minutes longer or until fish flakes easily when tested with a fork and bacon is browned. Yield: 4 servings.

Bass Fillets in White Wine

4 potatoes, parboiled and sliced
1/2 teaspoon chervil
1/2 teaspoon tarragon leaves
1/2 teaspoon chopped chives
Salt and pepper to taste
4 large bass fillets
1 cup dry white wine
1 cup buttered breadcrumbs

Arrange potato slices in a buttered, shallow baking dish. Combine chervil, tarragon, and chives; sprinkle over potatoes. Season with salt and pepper. Arrange fish on top; add salt and pepper to taste.

Pour wine over fish; cover with breadcrumbs. Bake at 400° for 30 minutes. Yield: 4 servings.

Shrimp-Stuffed Bass

1 (3- to 4-pound) bass, cleaned and dressed
Salt and pepper
1/3 cup chopped green pepper
1/2 cup chopped onion
1/4 cup chopped celery
6 tablespoons melted butter or margarine
1-3/4 cups soft breadcrumbs
12 medium shrimp, cooked, peeled, and deveined
1/2 cup chopped parsley
1/2 cup water
About 1 tablespoon butter or margarine
Lemon juice
Lemon wedges
Celery leaves (optional)

Dry fish thoroughly. Lay fish flat on a cutting board; slit lengthwise down center of fish to tail. Cut flesh along both sides of backbone to the tail, allowing the knife to run along the rib bones to form a pocket for the stuffing. Sprinkle both sides of pocket with salt and pepper to taste.

Sauté green pepper, onion, and celery in melted butter 5 minutes. Add breadcrumbs, shrimp, parsley, water, 1/2 teaspoon salt, and pepper to taste; mix lightly, but thoroughly. Stuff fish with shrimp mixture.

Place stuffed fish on a lightly buttered sheet of heavy-duty aluminum foil; loosely crush foil around edge of fish. Dot fish with butter, and sprinkle with lemon juice.

Bake at 400° about 30 minutes or until fish flakes easily when tested with a fork. Serve with lemon wedges; garnish with celery leaves, if desired. Yield: 4 to 6 servings.

Note: A dozen oysters may be substituted for shrimp; cut oysters in half. Reserve oyster liquid; add water to equal 1/2 cup, and substitute for 1/2 cup water.

Japanese kitchen scene, Okura Shukokan Museum, Tokyo; courtesy Bradley Smith

Provolone-Parmesan Stuffed Sole

6 tablespoons butter or margarine, divided
1/2 cup chopped green onion
1 cup shredded provolone cheese, divided
3/4 cup grated Parmesan cheese, divided
1/2 cup breadcrumbs
1-1/3 cups whipping cream, divided
2 pounds frozen sole fillets, thawed
2/3 cup dry white wine
1/4 cup all-purpose flour
1 tablespoon basil
1/2 teaspoon salt
1/8 teaspoon pepper
1/4 teaspoon oregano

Melt 2 tablespoons butter in a small saucepan; sauté onion 2 minutes, and set aside.

Combine 1/2 cup provolone cheese, 1/2 cup Parmesan cheese, breadcrumbs, and 1/3 cup whipping cream; spread on skin side of fillets. Roll up each fillet, and arrange in a shallow 2-quart baking dish. Pour wine over fish; sprinkle sautéed onion on top. Cover dish with brown paper, and bake at 350° for 25 minutes.

Pour off liquid from baking dish; simmer liquid in a medium saucepan until it is reduced to 1 cup. Melt 4 tablespoons butter in another medium saucepan. Blend in flour; place over low heat and stir until bubbly. Add fish liquid; cook, stirring constantly, until thickened.

Stir in 1 cup whipping cream, 1/2 cup provolone cheese, and 1/4 cup Parmesan cheese; cook, stirring constantly over medium heat until cheese melts. Do not boil.

Remove from heat; stir in basil, salt, pepper, and oregano. Pour sauce over fish. Yield: 8 servings.

Salmon Croquettes Supreme

1 (15-1/2-ounce) can red or pink salmon
2 eggs, beaten
1 cup toasted breadcrumbs
1/2 cup shredded Cheddar cheese
Salt and pepper to taste
Onion salt to taste
All-purpose flour
Hot vegetable oil

Drain salmon; remove skin and bones. Flake salmon with a fork. Add remaining ingredients except flour and oil, blending well; shape mixture into croquettes. Coat with flour. Pan fry in hot oil until golden brown, turning only once. Yield: 6 servings.

John A. Woodside: **Country Fair,** *1824, Collection of H. T. Peters, Jr., Virginia*

Cheeses

In 1824, when John A. Woodside, of Philadelphia, painted *Country Fair*, opposite, with its abundance of dairy cows, fat pigs, and handsome horses, most American country households made their own butter and cheese. It was all part of the weekly routine. Eliza Leslie, author of *Directions for Cookery*, published in 1828, advised housewives to "place the cheeses in the haystack and keep them there among the hay for five or six weeks. This is said to greatly improve their consistency and flavor. Cheeses are sometimes ripened by putting them every day in fresh grass." The Pennsylvania Dutch—Germans, actually—who lived in the part of Pennsylvania where this fair was held were excellent cheesemakers. One of them, Emil Frey, created Leiderkranz, in 1892. According to Waverley Root's history of American eating habits, it is one of the two cheeses of indisputable American origin. The other is brick cheese, first made in 1877 in Wisconsin. (Cheddar, of course, was an English invention.) Another German-American, whose name happened to be J.H. Kraft, came up with the notion of pre-packaging cheese. He sliced it and wrapped it in tinfoil, and eventually became a millionaire. France is probably the preeminent cheesemaking nation of the world: the varieties of French cheese fill an encyclopedia, and, as with French wines, only a connoisseur can know them all. Yet the United States is the largest cheese producer in the world. A few of our home-cured varieties are at right.

Cheese crêpes with wine sauce surrounded by Camembert, Jarlsberg, Parmesan, Cheddar, and other cheeses. Photographed by Jerome Drown.

Cheese

The versatility of cheese extends to snack, sandwich, soufflé, and even soup. Eugene Field, American poet, found yet another use for the wonderful stuff:

> No matter what conditions . . .
> The best of all physicians
>   Is apple pie and cheese!

Cheese Crêpes with Wine Sauce

1-1/4 cups all-purpose flour
Pinch of salt
3 eggs, beaten
1-1/2 cups milk
2 tablespoons melted butter or margarine
Vegetable oil
Cheese filling (recipe follows)
Wine sauce (recipe follows)
Parsley sprigs (optional)

Combine flour, salt, and eggs; mix well. Add milk and butter; beat until smooth. Refrigerate batter at least 2 hours (this allows flour particles to swell and soften so the crêpes are light in texture).

Brush the bottom of a 6- or 7-inch crêpe pan or heavy skillet with vegetable oil; place pan over medium heat until vegetable oil is just hot, but not smoking.

Pour 2 to 3 tablespoons batter into pan; quickly tilt pan in all directions so batter covers the pan in a thin film. Cook about 1 minute.

Lift edge of crêpe to test for doneness. Crêpe is ready for flipping when it can be shaken loose from pan. Flip the crêpe, and cook about 30 seconds on the other side.

When the crêpes are done, stack them between layers of waxed paper to prevent sticking.

Place 1 heaping tablespoonful cheese filling in center of each crêpe; roll up, tucking in ends.

Place crêpes seam side down, in a lightly greased shallow baking dish. Bake at 400° for 20 minutes.

Spoon wine sauce over the crêpes; garnish with parsley, if desired. Yield: 12 servings.

Cheese Filling:
6 tablespoons butter or margarine
1/2 cup all-purpose flour
2 cups milk
3 to 4 ounces Gruyère cheese, shredded
1/2 (2-ounce) package sapsago cheese, grated
3 egg yolks, beaten
Freshly ground pepper to taste
Grated nutmeg to taste

Melt butter in a heavy saucepan over low heat; add flour, and cook, stirring, 1 minute. Add milk; cook, stirring, until thickened. Add cheese, stirring until cheese melts.

Stir 2 to 3 tablespoons cheese mixture into egg yolks. Gradually add egg mixture to cheese mixture; mix well. Stir in pepper and nutmeg. Pour into a 9-inch square baking pan to cool. Chill 3 to 4 hours before using. Yield: 3 cups.

Wine Sauce:
3 tablespoons butter or margarine
3 tablespoons all-purpose flour
1 cup chicken broth
1 cup dry white wine
2 tablespoons whipping cream
1 egg yolk
Salt and pepper to taste
2 tablespoons finely chopped parsley
1/4 cup sautéed sliced mushrooms (optional)

Melt butter in a heavy saucepan; add flour, blending until smooth. Stir in broth; cook over medium heat until smooth and thickened, stirring constantly. Remove from heat; add wine.

Combine cream and egg yolk, mixing well; stir in a small amount of wine sauce. Add egg mixture to remaining wine sauce; cook, stirring, until smooth and thick. Season with salt and pepper. Add parsley; stir in mushrooms if desired. Cook 1 minute. Yield: 2-1/2 cups.

Blue Cheese Salad Dressing

2 cups mayonnaise
1 teaspoon lemon juice
1 teaspoon white vinegar
1/4 cup buttermilk
1/2 cup commercial sour cream
1/2 teaspoon salt
1/4 teaspoon pepper
1/4 teaspoon garlic powder
1 (4-ounce) package blue cheese, crumbled

Combine all ingredients except blue cheese; blend well. Gently stir in blue cheese. Refrigerate until needed. Yield: about 3 cups.

Cheddar Soufflé

1/4 cup plus 2 tablespoons butter or margarine, melted
1/4 cup plus 2 tablespoons all-purpose flour
1 teaspoon salt
1/2 teaspoon paprika
Dash of cayenne
1-1/2 cups milk
6 ounces Cheddar cheese, cubed (1-1/2 cups)
6 large eggs, separated

Cut a piece of waxed paper or aluminum foil long enough to fit around a 2-quart soufflé dish, allowing a 1-inch overlap; fold lengthwise into thirds. (Aluminum foil should be buttered.)

Wrap waxed paper around dish, allowing paper to extend 2 inches above rim of dish to form a collar. Secure ends with tape; butter soufflé dish, and set aside.

Combine butter, flour, and seasonings in a medium saucepan; cook over medium heat until bubbly. Gradually add milk; cook over medium heat, stirring constantly, until thickened. Add cheese, stirring until melted; remove from heat.

Beat egg yolks until thick and lemon colored; gradually stir into cheese mixture. Beat egg whites until stiff but not dry; fold into cheese mixture. Pour into soufflé dish; bake at 350° for 45 minutes. Serve immediately. Yield: 6 to 8 servings.

Creamy Cheesecake Dessert

1 (24-ounce) carton cottage cheese
1-1/2 cups milk
5 eggs
1 teaspoon vanilla extract
1/4 teaspoon almond extract
1/4 teaspoon salt
1 cup sugar
3/4 cup all-purpose flour
Strawberry jam
Whipped cream

Combine cottage cheese and milk in container of electric blender; process until smooth. Add eggs, flavorings, and salt; process until well blended. Combine sugar and flour; add to cheese mixture and blend thoroughly.

Pour mixture into a buttered 9-inch square pan, and set in a pan of water. Bake at 350° for 1 hour or until a knife inserted halfway between edge and center of pan comes out clean. Cool.

Before serving, top with strawberry jam and whipped cream. Yield: about 9 servings.

Roquefort and Apple Omelet

2 tart apples, peeled, cored, and sliced
3 tablespoons melted butter or margarine, divided
5 eggs, beaten
2 tablespoons milk
2 to 3 tablespoons grated Parmesan cheese
Salt and pepper to taste
1/2 cup (2 ounces) crumbled Roquefort cheese

Sauté apples in 2 tablespoons butter 1 minute in a heavy skillet; remove from skillet, and set aside.

Combine eggs, milk, Parmesan cheese, salt, and pepper; beat well. Add 1 tablespoon butter to skillet, and heat until hot enough to sizzle a drop of water. Pour in egg mixture, all at once.

With a fork, lift cooked portions of egg mixture at edges so uncooked portion flows underneath. When omelet is set and egg mixture no longer flows freely, remove from heat. (It will be moist and creamy on top.)

Sprinkle Roquefort cheese and half of sautéed apple wedges on one side of omelet; fold in half. Transfer to a warm dish, and garnish with remaining apple wedges. Serve immediately. Yield: 2 to 3 servings.

Golden Cheese Chowder

3 cups water
4 medium potatoes, cubed
1 cup sliced celery
1 cup sliced carrots
1/2 cup diced onion
2 teaspoons salt
1/4 teaspoon pepper
1/2 cup butter or margarine
1/2 cup all-purpose flour
4 cups milk
1 pound sharp Cheddar cheese, shredded
2 cups cubed cooked ham
Hot sauce

Bring water to a boil in a Dutch oven, and add vegetables, salt, and pepper. Cover; lower heat, and simmer 10 minutes or until vegetables are done.

Melt butter in a large saucepan. Blend in flour, and gradually stir in milk. Cook over medium heat, stirring constantly, until mixture comes to a boil; boil for 1 minute. Add cheese, and stir until melted.

Stir cheese mixture into vegetables. Add ham and hot sauce to taste, stirring well. Heat thoroughly, but do not boil. Yield: 12 servings.

Calico Cheese Soup

1/2 clove garlic
1/4 cup vegetable oil
1/2 cup finely chopped carrots
1/2 cup finely chopped celery
Boiling water
2 tablespoons minced onion
4 tablespoons butter or margarine
3 tablespoons all-purpose flour
2 cups milk, scalded
2 cups chicken broth
2 cups shredded Cheddar cheese
2 cups medium bread cubes
1/4 cup grated Parmesan cheese

Soak garlic in vegetable oil 2 to 3 hours; set aside. Place carrots and celery in boiling, salted water to cover; cover and cook just until crisp-tender. Drain and set aside.

Sauté onion in butter until tender. Stir in flour, milk, and chicken broth, blending well. Cook, stirring constantly, until slightly thickened. Add cheese; stir until melted. Add vegetable mixture; cook 10 minutes.

Toast bread cubes until golden brown. Remove garlic from oil. Combine oil and Parmesan cheese; toss with croutons. Serve on top of hot soup. Yield: 4 to 6 servings.

Welsh Rarebit

1 tablespoon butter or margarine
1 pound sharp Cheddar cheese, cut into
    1/2-inch cubes
3/4 to 1 cup milk or beer
1 teaspoon Worcestershire sauce
1/2 teaspoon salt
1/2 teaspoon paprika
1/2 teaspoon dry mustard
Dash of red pepper
1 egg, beaten
6 tomato slices
6 slices bread, toasted
6 slices bacon, cooked and halved

Combine butter and cheese in top of a double boiler; stir until cheese is melted. Gradually stir in milk; add Worcestershire sauce, salt, paprika, mustard, and pepper. Stir in egg. Cook until slightly thickened, stirring constantly.

To serve, pour cheese sauce into a chafing dish. Place a tomato slice on each slice of bread; top each tomato with 2 bacon halves. Spoon cheese sauce over bacon, and serve immediately. Yield: 6 servings.

A nineteenth-century American stoneware butter churn from the Henry Ford Museum in Dearborn, Michigan. The word Lyons on the neck of the churn is probably the town of origin, but might well be the name of the craftsman who made it.

Cheese Crock

1 pound sharp Cheddar cheese, shredded
1 (3-ounce) package cream cheese
2 tablespoons olive oil
1-1/2 teaspoons dry mustard
1-1/4 teaspoons minced garlic
3 tablespoons brandy

Let cheeses stand at room temperature until soft; blend together until very smooth. Add olive oil, mustard, garlic, and brandy, blending well. Pack into a stoneware cheese crock; cover and refrigerate at least 1 week before serving. To serve, allow cheese to soften at room temperature 1 hour; serve on crackers, melba toast, or party rye bread. Yield: about 3 cups.

Note: Cheese can be kept going as long as part of the original mixture is left. To add to crock, any firm cheese such as Cheddar, Swiss, Jack, etc. may be used. Shred any cheese scraps and blend with a small amount of cream cheese and olive oil until smooth; add beer, sherry, kirsch, or brandy, keeping the original proportion the same. Let mixture age a few days before serving again.

Benin style, Nigeria: Bronze Cock, 18th century, National Gallery of Art, Washington, D.C.

Fowl Play and Fair

Useful, delectable, versatile, nourishing, and thoroughly admirable as barnyard fowl may be, they have failed to arouse much poetry in the human heart. Nor have they inspired many artists. And yet whoever made the gorgeously carved and caparisoned bronze cock, opposite, must surely have thought him a noble beast even if he was a chicken. The sculpture was made in the West African kingdom of Benin sometime in the eighteenth century, when the artists of that land were producing some of the finest bronzes ever created. Chickens and other fowl have seldom been granted such attention in European and American art. A few turn up in poetry. There is, of course, Mother Goose, and in her book of rhymes are a number of exemplary little hens. One of them washes dishes, cleans house, brings tankards of ale from the cellar, and sits telling stories by the fireside. Another is the higgledy-piggledy black hen, laying eggs for gentlemen. Besides Mother Goose, there is the following celebrated limerick:

> The Reverend Henry Ward Beecher
> Called a hen a most elegant creature.
> Then the hen, pleased with that,
> Laid an egg in his hat,
> And thus did the hen reward Beecher.

In a hundred other ways does the hen reward us—as in the recipes for the Cornish hens at right and other dishes that follow.

Cornish Hens à l'Orange photographed by Taylor Lewis

Fowl

On the occasion, we gather together for turkey or Christmas goose, but the basic bird —in farm kitchen or four-star restaurant—is the chicken.

Chicken Breasts Cordon Bleu

4 large chicken breasts, split, boned, and skinned
Salt and pepper to taste
4 thin slices boiled ham, halved
4 slices natural Swiss cheese, halved
1 egg
2 to 3 tablespoons water
1/2 cup fine breadcrumbs
1/2 cup all-purpose flour
1/2 cup grated Parmesan cheese
Melted butter or margarine
Hot vegetable oil
Creamy Sauce

Place each half of chicken breast on waxed paper; carefully flatten to 1/4-inch thickness, using a meat mallet or rolling pin. Sprinkle chicken with salt and pepper. Place 1/2 slice of ham and cheese on each half of chicken breast; tuck in sides and roll up jellyroll fashion. Secure with toothpick or tie securely.

Combine egg and water; beat well. Combine breadcrumbs, flour, and Parmesan cheese. Dip each piece of chicken in egg; then coat with breadcrumb mixture. Cook in mixture of butter and oil until tender. (Reserve pan drippings for use in Creamy Sauce.) Serve with Creamy Sauce. Yield: 8 servings.

Creamy Sauce:
2 tablespoons all-purpose flour
Reserved pan drippings
3/4 cup chicken broth
1/4 cup dry white wine

Blend flour into pan drippings; cook over low heat until bubbly. Gradually blend in broth and wine; cook, stirring constantly, until smooth and thickened. Yield: 1 cup.

Country Captain

3-1/2 to 4 pounds chicken thighs, legs, and boned breasts
All-purpose flour
Salt and pepper to taste
1 cup shortening
2 onions, finely chopped
2 green peppers, chopped
1 small clove garlic, minced
1-1/2 teaspoons salt
1/2 teaspoon white pepper
3 teaspoons curry powder
2 (16-ounce) cans tomato wedges, undrained
1/2 teaspoon chopped parsley
1/2 teaspoon ground thyme
3 heaping tablespoons currants
Hot cooked rice
1/4 pound slivered almonds, toasted
Parsley for garnish

Remove skin from chicken. Combine flour and salt and pepper to taste. Dredge chicken in flour mixture, and brown in hot shortening. Remove chicken from skillet, but keep it hot (this step is important for the success of the dish).

Pour off all but 1/4 cup drippings from skillet. Add onion, green pepper, and garlic; cook very slowly, stirring constantly, until vegetables are tender. Season with 1-1/2 teaspoons salt, 1/2 teaspoon white pepper, and curry powder (amount of curry powder may be varied according to taste). Add tomatoes, 1/2 teaspoon parsley, thyme, and currants; stir gently to mix.

Put chicken in a roaster or large casserole; add sauce. If sauce does not cover chicken, add water. Cover tightly and bake at 350° about 45 minutes or until the chicken is tender.

Place chicken in center of a large platter and pile rice around it. Spoon sauce over rice; sprinkle almonds on top. Yield: 8 to 10 servings.

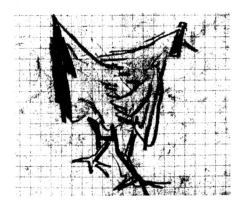

Sketch of a hen by van Gogh. National Museum, Amsterdam

Chicken Niçoise

2 (3-pound) chickens, cut in serving-size pieces
About 2 tablespoons olive oil
1 clove garlic, chopped
2 tablespoons freeze-dried chopped shallots
1 onion, diced
1 cup white wine
1 small eggplant, peeled and diced
3 zucchini, sliced
3 ripe tomatoes, quartered

Sauté chicken in olive oil. Add garlic, shallots, onion, and wine; cover and simmer 20 minutes. Add eggplant, zucchini, and tomatoes; simmer about 25 minutes or until chicken and vegetables are tender. Yield: 6 servings.

Tempura Fried Chicken

4 whole chicken breasts, halved and boned
1 egg
Milk
1/2 cup tempura batter mix
1/2 teaspoon salt
1/4 teaspoon pepper
1/2 cup peanut oil

Cut each half of chicken breast into 4 strips. Break egg into measuring cup; add enough milk to make 1/2 cup. Stir egg and milk into tempura batter mix; add salt and pepper. Dip chicken into batter; brown in hot oil in tempura pan. Yield: 4 to 6 servings.

Note: When frying chicken, leave a few strips of chicken in pan before adding additional strips; the chicken left in the pan will absorb the heat of the oil and keep it from overheating.

Cornish Hens Teriyaki

1/2 cup melted butter or margarine
4 cups seasoned croutons
1/2 cup diced mandarin orange sections
8 Cornish hens
1/2 cup soy sauce
2 cloves garlic, crushed

Combine margarine, croutons, and mandarin orange sections; mix well. Place hens, breast side up, in a shallow roasting pan; stuff with crouton mixture.

Combine soy sauce and garlic; brush on hens. Bake at 350° about 1 hour, basting every 15 minutes with pan drippings. Yield: 8 servings.

Cornish Hens à l'orange

8 Cornish hens
4 oranges, peeled and sliced
1-1/2 cups orange juice
1-1/2 teaspoons salt
1/4 teaspoon pepper
1/2 cup firmly packed brown sugar
Hot wild rice
4 oranges, halved
4 teaspoons cranberry sauce

Rinse cavity and outside of hens. Fill cavity of each hen with orange slices. Sew or skewer opening. Place hens, breast side up, in a roasting pan. Combine orange juice, salt, pepper, and brown sugar to make basting sauce. Roast hens uncovered at 450° for 15 minutes, brushing with basting mixture three times.

Reduce oven temperature to 350° and roast 30 minutes longer, basting once or twice.

At end of baking time, remove skewers and orange stuffing (discard stuffing). Serve with hot wild rice, and garnish with orange halves with a dab of cranberry sauce in center of each. Yield: 8 servings.

Holiday Roast Goose

3 cups chopped apple
3/4 cup melted butter or margarine
6 cups toasted breadcrumbs
1-1/2 cups chopped onion
1 tablespoon salt
1 tablespoon celery seeds
1 tablespoon pepper
3/4 cup apple cider
1 (10-pound) dressed goose
Salt and pepper
Green grapes

Cook apples in butter until transparent; add breadcrumbs, onion, and seasonings; toss lightly. Add cider, and mix well.

Lightly rub goose with salt and pepper inside and out. Stuff the body and neck cavity loosely with apple stuffing; truss goose. Prick breast, legs, and wings of goose to allow fat to run out; place breast side up on rack in shallow roasting pan.

Roast, uncovered, at 325° for 4 to 5 hours or until an internal temperature of 180° to 185° is reached. Do not baste. Spoon off drippings every half hour.

Goose is done when drumsticks and thighs move easily or when juices run clear instead of pink if thigh is pricked with a fork. Serve on a platter garnished with grapes. Yield: 10 to 15 servings.

Quick and Easy Turkey Divan

2 (10-ounce) packages frozen broccoli spears
2 cups diced cooked turkey
1 (6-ounce) package process American cheese slices
1 (13-ounce) can evaporated milk
1 (10-3/4-ounce) can condensed cream of mushroom soup, undiluted
1 (3-ounce) can fried onion rings

Place broccoli in a small amount of water and bring to a boil; cover and simmer 3 minutes. Drain and set aside. Arrange turkey in a greased 11-1/2- x 7-1/2- x 1-1/2-inch baking dish; top with broccoli. Place cheese over broccoli.

Combine milk and soup, and pour over cheese.

Bake at 350° for 25 minutes; remove from oven and sprinkle with onion rings. Bake 5 additional minutes. Yield: 8 to 10 servings.

Cornish Hens Veronique

4 (1-pound) Cornish hens
Salt
1/4 cup melted butter or margarine
1 (8-ounce) can light seedless grapes
3 tablespoons sugar
1/4 cup Sauterne
2 tablespoons lemon juice
1 tablespoon cornstarch
1/4 teaspoon salt
1/4 teaspoon grated orange peel
1/4 teaspoon grated lemon peel
Fresh seedless grape clusters (optional)

Sprinkle cavity of hens with salt; truss hens, and place breast side up in a shallow roasting pan. Cover loosely with aluminum foil; bake at 375° for 30 minutes.

Remove aluminum foil. Bake at 375° for an additional 15 minutes, basting frequently with butter.

Drain grapes, reserving liquid; set grapes aside. Heat sugar in a heavy saucepan over medium heat until melted and deep golden brown. Remove from heat, and set aside.

Bring reserved grape liquid to a boil in a small saucepan; gradually stir into caramelized sugar. Place over medium heat; cook, stirring constantly, until caramel dissolves.

Combine Sauterne, lemon juice, cornstarch, 1/4 teaspoon salt, and citrus peel; stir into syrup mixture. Cook, stirring constantly, until mixture thickens and bubbles; stir in reserved grapes.

Bake hens at 375° an additional 15 minutes, basting frequently with syrup mixture. Garnish with grape clusters, if desired. Yield: 4 servings.

Smoked Duck with Gourmet Rice

1/2 cup lemon juice
1/2 cup soy sauce
1/2 teaspoon salt
1/4 teaspoon coarsely ground black pepper
1/4 teaspoon paprika
1/8 teaspoon garlic salt
1 (4- to 5-pound) duck
8 cloves
2 onions
Gourmet Rice
Parsley

Combine lemon juice, soy sauce, salt, pepper, paprika, and garlic salt; pour over duck, and marinate in refrigerator several hours. Stick 4 cloves in each onion, and place in duck cavity. Place duck on rack in smoker. (Use smoker with water pan.)

Cook about 5 hours in smoker. Do not raise lid; allow duck to cook slowly without being disturbed until very crisp.

If you do not have a smoker, duck can be cooked in the oven at 325° for 2 hours. Serve duck on bed of Gourmet Rice. Garnish with parsley. Yield: 4 servings.

Gourmet Rice:
4 cloves
1 onion
1 duck heart, liver, kidney, and neck
1 carrot
2 stalks celery with leaves
Salt to taste
1 teaspoon peppercorns
1 bay leaf
1 clove garlic
About 1/4 teaspoon red pepper seeds
About 4 sprigs parsley
1 cup uncooked regular rice
1/2 cup diced celery
1/4 cup chopped scallions
1/2 cup sliced mushrooms
2 tablespoons melted butter

Stick cloves in onion; combine with next 9 ingredients. Cover with water, and cook until meat is tender. Remove meat and vegetables from broth; discard vegetables, and chop meat. Strain broth, reserving 2 cups.

Cook rice in reserved broth over low heat about 25 minutes or until tender. Sauté diced celery, scallions, and mushrooms in butter; add to rice along with chopped meat, tossing lightly to mix. Yield: 4 servings.

Paul Cézanne: Still Life with Apples and Peaches, *1905, National Gallery of Art, Washington, D.C.*

An August Gathering

It is nothing much, at first glance. A few pieces of fruit, a pitcher, a bowl, and a kitchen towel on a table. Yet, as with any other canvas by Paul Cézanne, it is generally conceded to be a masterpiece, almost beyond price. During Cézanne's lifetime, his work was more often than not rejected and ridiculed. Though he never lost his determination to continue painting ("There is only one living painter—myself," he once said), even he might be astonished if he had lived to see how high his reputation would rise—among both painters and the public. In fact, he has been called the father of modern art.

Cézanne was born in 1839 in the old French town of Aix-en-Provence, the son of a successful banker. Instead of following his father's lead, he began to paint. He went around in outlandish clothing, took a mistress, and seemed doomed to amount to nothing. After spending some time in Paris, where he became acquainted with the leading Impressionist painters of the day, he returned to Provence and lived almost as a hermit. His pictures are never "pretty." He invariably took the simplest, most commonplace things as his subjects, and endowed them with a universal gravity, an atomic weight. His intention, he said, was to make of Impressionism "something solid and durable like the art of the museums." His still-lifes glow with light, but they are solid and durable as the earth.

The pleasures of fresh fruit, like the pleasures of Cézanne's paintings, are simple and direct—and, above all, visual. Fruit just picked from the orchard, as in the scene at right, is wonderful to look at and a feast in itself. The fruits that one finds year-round in the market are often better used in cooking—in salads, compotes, cobblers, pies, and even soups.

Summer fruits photographed by Taylor Lewis

Fruit

"A plum of a job," "the apple of my eye," "peachy-keen!" and even the hybrid theatrical-tropical "top banana" use fruit as a metaphor for excellence. Exception: "Our new car is a lemon." Here are some recipes which "are the berries."

Orange Salad Bowl

8 cups torn salad greens
2 cups orange sections
1 cup pecans or peanuts, chopped
1 onion, sliced and separated into rings
Celery Seed Dressing
    Combine first four ingredients, and toss gently with Celery Seed Dressing. Yield: 8 servings.

Celery Seed Dressing:
1/3 cup sugar
1 teaspoon salt
1 teaspoon dry mustard
1/3 cup vinegar
1 small onion, chopped
1 cup vegetable oil
1 tablespoon celery seeds
    Combine all ingredients, mixing well. Chill thoroughly before serving. Yield: 1-1/3 cups.

Nutty Cranberries

1 cup sugar
2 cups orange juice
1 (1-pound) bag fresh cranberries
2 cups walnut halves or pieces
    Dissolve sugar in orange juice in a medium saucepan over low heat. Add cranberries, and bring mixture to a boil; let boil 3 to 5 minutes. Stir in walnuts, and remove from heat. Cool. Yield: 10 to 12 servings.

Rum-Broiled Grapefruit

1 large grapefruit, halved
1 teaspoon dark rum
2 tablespoons apricot or peach preserves
1 tablespoon melted butter
    Remove seeds and loosen sections of each grapefruit half; sprinkle 1/2 teaspoon rum over top of each.
    Combine preserves and butter, mixing well; spread evenly over grapefruit halves. Broil grapefruit 4 inches from heat 3 to 5 minutes or until bubbly. Yield: 2 servings.

Minted Grapefruit

4 cups fresh grapefruit sections
1/3 cup crème de menthe
Mint sprigs
    Combine grapefruit sections and crème de menthe, stirring to coat well. Refrigerate several hours. Spoon into sherbet glasses, and garnish with mint. Yield: 6 servings.

Rich Peach Ice Cream

1 quart whipping cream
2-1/2 cups sugar, divided
3 cups finely chopped ripe peaches
Pinch of salt
    Scald whipping cream and 1-1/4 cups sugar in top of a double boiler, stirring to dissolve sugar. Pour mixture into a 1/2-gallon hand-turned or electric freezer; freeze until thickened.
    Puree peaches by mashing or by processing in container of electric blender. Combine 1-1/4 cups sugar, salt, and peach puree; stir until sugar dissolves. Remove dasher; stir pureed mixture into custard. Return dasher, and freeze until firm. Let ripen 1 hour before serving. Yield: 1/2 gallon.

Citrus Combo

2 grapefruit, peeled, seeded, and sectioned
3 oranges, peeled, seeded, and sectioned
3 tangerines, peeled, seeded, and sectioned
1/2 cup sugar, divided
1/2 cup shredded coconut, divided
    Place half the fruit in a bowl; sprinkle with 1/4 cup sugar and 1/4 cup coconut. Repeat layers. Chill at least 1 hour. Yield: 8 servings.

Swedish Fruit Soup

1 (8-ounce) package mixed dried fruits, cut into bite-size pieces
2-1/2 cups water
1/2 teaspoon ground cinnamon
1 (3-ounce) package cherry-flavored gelatin
3 cups orange juice
Commercial sour cream
    Combine dried fruit, water, and cinnamon in a large saucepan; bring to a boil. Cover; reduce heat, and simmer 20 minutes.
    Remove from heat, and stir in gelatin until dissolved; add orange juice. Chill.
    Serve soup cold, topped with sour cream. Yield: about 8 servings.

Curried Fruit

1 (16-ounce) can sliced peaches, drained
1 (16-ounce) can pear halves, drained
1 (17-ounce) can apricot halves, drained
1 (16-ounce) can pitted dark sweet cherries, drained
1 (15-1/2-ounce) can pineapple chunks, drained
2/3 cup slivered almonds
3/4 cup firmly packed light brown sugar
2 to 3 teaspoons curry powder
1/3 cup melted butter or margarine
    Layer fruit in a 13- x 9- x 2-inch baking dish; sprinkle with almonds. Combine brown sugar and curry powder; stir in melted butter, and spoon over fruit. Bake at 325° for 1 hour; cool. Refrigerate overnight; bake fruit at 350° for 20 minutes or until bubbly. Yield: 8 servings.

A 19th century engraving of a family gathering apples. New York Public Library

Crusty Apple Delight

1-1/2 cups sugar, divided
1 cup all-purpose flour
1/2 cup butter or margarine, softened
3 cups peeled, sliced apple
Ground cinnamon
Whipped cream or ice cream (optional)

Combine 1 cup sugar and flour. Using 2 knives or a pastry blender, cut butter into flour mixture until crumbly; set aside.

Place a layer of apple slices in a buttered 8-inch square baking dish. Sprinkle with some of remaining sugar; add cinnamon to taste. Repeat this procedure until all apple slices are used. Place crumb mixture on top of apple slices, patting until apples are covered. Bake at 350° for 30 minutes or until golden brown. Top with whipped cream, if desired. Yield: about 6 servings.

Island Fruit Boats

3 fresh pineapples
4 oranges, peeled and sectioned
4 unpeeled apples, cut into wedges
1 cup sliced celery
1 (6-ounce) can frozen lemonade concentrate, thawed and undiluted

Cut pineapples in half lengthwise; scoop out pulp, leaving shells intact. Cut pineapple pulp into chunks, and set aside 2 cups (use remaining pineapple chunks as desired).

Combine 2 cups pineapple with remaining ingredients; chill well. Drain and spoon into pineapple shells. Yield: 6 to 8 servings.

Papaya Boats

2 medium papayas
1 (8-1/4-ounce) can pineapple chunks, undrained
2 bananas, sliced
2 oranges, peeled and sectioned
1 cup sugar

Cut papayas in half; scoop out seeds with a spoon. Remove pulp, using a melon ball scoop, leaving shells intact; set aside shells.

Combine papaya balls and remaining ingredients. Fill papaya shells with fruit mixture; chill well. Yield: about 4 servings.

An early woodcut of a pineapple NYPL

Tropical Fruit Salad

2 mangoes
3 bananas, sliced
Lemon juice
3 apples, chopped
1 orange, sectioned and seeded
1 kiwi, peeled and sliced
3 to 4 tablespoons sugar
Whipped cream

Cut mangoes in half; remove seeds with a spoon. Scoop out pulp with a melon ball scoop, leaving shells intact; set aside shells.

Dip banana slices in lemon juice to prevent darkening.

Combine mango, bananas, apples, orange, kiwi, and sugar; chill several hours. Spoon chilled mixture into mango shells, and serve with whipped cream. Yield: 4 servings.

Cold Spiced Fruit

1 to 2 unpeeled oranges, sliced and seeded
1 (20-ounce) can pineapple chunks
1 (16-ounce) can sliced peaches
1 (16-ounce) can apricot halves
1 (29-ounce) can pears
1 cup sugar
1/2 cup vinegar
3 sticks cinnamon
5 whole cloves
1 (3-ounce) package cherry-flavored gelatin

Cut orange slices in half; place in a saucepan and cover with water. Simmer until rind is tender; drain well and set aside.

Drain canned fruits well, reserving all of the pineapple juice and half of the peach and apricot juice.

Combine reserved juice, sugar, vinegar, cinnamon, cloves, and gelatin; simmer 30 minutes. Combine fruits in a 9-cup container; pour hot juice mixture over fruit. Refrigerate at least 24 hours. Yield: about 15 servings.

Peach Fried Pies

2 (8-ounce) packages dried peaches
1/2 to 3/4 cup sugar
2 tablespoons lemon juice
1/2 teaspoon ground cinnamon
1/2 teaspoon ground nutmeg
Egg Pastry
Vegetable oil

Cover peaches with boiling water, and cook until very tender (about 30 minutes). Drain, reserving 1/4 cup liquid; cool. Mash peaches, and combine with reserved liquid, sugar, lemon juice, and spices; set aside.

Roll out pastry on waxed paper, one-third at a time. Cut out pastry circles, using a 5-inch saucer as a measure.

Place about 3 tablespoons of peach mixture on half of each pastry circle. To seal pies, dip fingers in water, and moisten edges of circles; fold in half, making sure edges are even. Using a fork dipped in flour, press pastry edges firmly together.

Heat 1 inch of vegetable oil to 375°. Cook pies until golden brown on both sides, turning only once. Drain well on paper towels. Yield: about 1-1/2 dozen.

Egg Pastry:
3 cups all-purpose flour
1 teaspoon salt
1 cup shortening
1 egg, beaten
4 tablespoons water
1 teaspoon vinegar

Combine flour and salt; cut in shortening until mixture resembles coarse cornmeal. Combine egg and water; sprinkle over flour mixture. Add vinegar, and lightly stir until mixture forms a ball.

Wrap pastry in waxed paper; chill at least 1 hour or until ready to use. Yield: pastry for about 1-1/2 dozen 5-inch pies.

Ambrosia

6 oranges, peeled and sectioned
1/2 cup sugar or to taste
1 coconut, grated

Place a layer of orange sections in a glass bowl; sprinkle with sugar, and layer with coconut. Repeat layers, ending with coconut. Chill. Yield: about 6 servings.

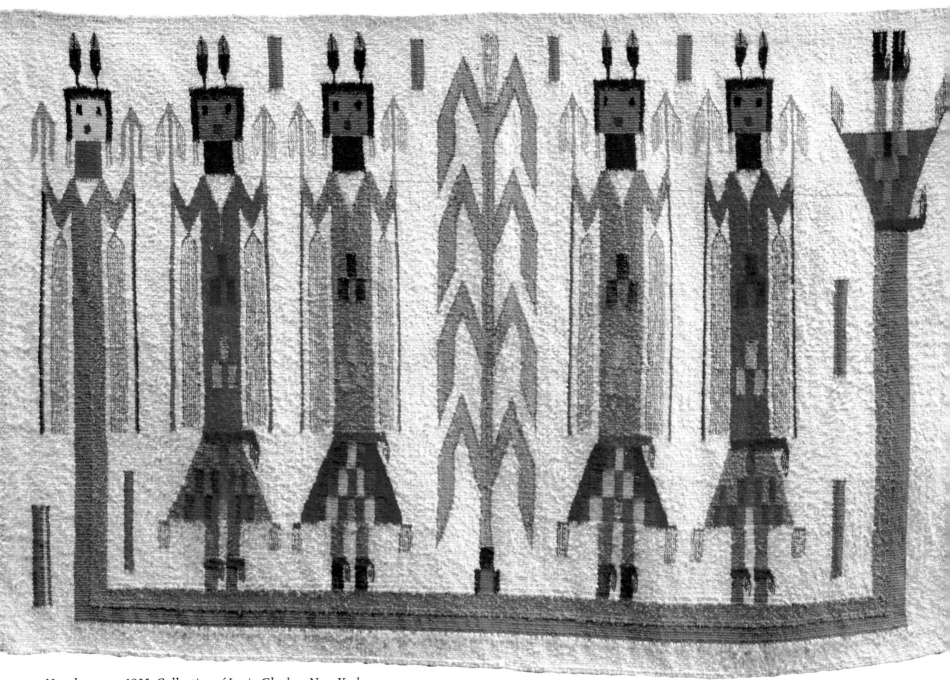

Navaho rug, c. 1955, Collection of Irwin Glusker, New York

Indian Gift

There is something miraculous about corn. It grows rapidly, and it is the tallest plant in the vegetable garden. Once harvested, it undergoes a string of magical permutations. It is hominy, popcorn, johnny-cake, tortillas, roasting ears, and (boiled down to its most potent essence) whiskey. No wonder that the great Indian civilizations of the Americas—whose people knew nothing about whiskey and drank corn beer instead—regarded corn as a god. Often a harsh god, too. Most of the citizens of ancient Peru, for example, spent their entire lives cultivating corn. The wealth and comfort of their society depended upon it. No one knows quite when or how, but wild corn was apparently domesticated somewhere in central Mexico, perhaps as far back as 6000 B. C.—long before the pyramids were built in Egypt, long before the time of Moses. Corn was unknown in Europe until Columbus brought it back from his first trip to Cuba. Once it was introduced, it remained a regional crop, flourishing mainly in Africa and around the Mediterranean Sea. The English settlers arriving in Jamestown in 1607 had never heard of it, but the Indians very obligingly showed them how to plant, preserve, grind, and cook the plant they called maize. Corn was on its way to becoming an American staple. The contemporary Navaho textile opposite evokes the origins of corn: it shows a group of women—themselves very like the cornstalk at center—in a cornfield. The fresh-picked ears and the jars of corn relish at right similarly evoke the long culinary history of this versatile grain.

Fresh corn and relish photographed by Jerome Brown

Corn

Indians introduced the first Southern colonists to cooking with corn. The settlers learned to grind the grain for bread and cakes, as well as to use the fresh kernels in chowders, relishes and main dishes. Processed, packaged, popped and—for a glorious few weeks every summer—fresh on the cob, this native grain now appears at every juncture of our national diet. We take it as real nourishment from the breakfast bowl and munch it as junk food in the movie theater.

Corn Fritters

3 eggs, separated
1 (12-ounce) can whole kernel corn, drained
1/4 cup all-purpose flour
1/2 teaspoon salt
1/4 teaspoon pepper
1/2 cup vegetable oil

Beat egg yolks well; stir in corn, flour, salt, and pepper. Fold in stiffly beaten egg whites. Drop batter by tablespoonfuls into oil heated to 375°. Cook until golden, turning once. Drain on paper towels. Yield: about 1 dozen.

Marinated Vegetable Salad

1 pound carrots, sliced and cooked
1 (12-ounce) can whole kernel corn, drained
1 (17-ounce) can green peas, drained
6 green onions, chopped
1 green pepper, chopped
1 (10-3/4-ounce) can tomato soup, undiluted
1 cup sugar
1/2 cup vegetable oil
1/4 cup cider vinegar
1 tablespoon Worcestershire sauce
1 teaspoon dry mustard

Combine first 5 ingredients; set aside. Combine remaining ingredients, mixing well. Pour over vegetables, and toss lightly. Refrigerate several hours or overnight. Yield: 10 to 12 servings.

Corn Soufflé

2 tablespoons minced green pepper
1/4 cup melted butter or margarine
2 tablespoons all-purpose flour
1-1/2 cups half-and-half, scalded
1/2 cup grated Parmesan cheese
3 egg yolks
1/2 cup cooked fresh corn
2 tablespoons chopped pimiento, drained well
1 teaspoon salt
Pinch of cream of tartar
4 egg whites (at room temperature)

Sauté green pepper in butter until tender; stir in flour. Gradually add half-and-half; cook, stirring constantly, until smooth and thickened. Add cheese, stirring until melted. Remove from heat; add egg yolks, one at a time, stirring well after each addition. Stir in corn, pimiento, and salt; allow mixture to cool 15 minutes.

Combine cream of tartar and egg whites in a large mixing bowl; beat until stiff but not dry. Fold beaten egg whites into corn mixture. Pour into an ungreased 1-1/2-quart casserole. Bake at 350° for 20 to 25 minutes or until golden brown. Yield: 4 to 5 servings.

Fresh Corn Salad

8 ears of fresh corn
1/2 cup olive oil
1/4 cup cider vinegar
1 tablespoon lemon juice
2 teaspoons Dijon mustard
1/4 teaspoon salt
1/8 teaspoon pepper
1/4 cup snipped parsley
2 teaspoons basil or tarragon leaves
2 large tomatoes, peeled and chopped
1 small green pepper, cut into strips
1/2 cup minced green onion
Lettuce (optional)

Drop corn into boiling salted water to cover. Return to a boil; cover and cook 10 minutes or until tender. Drain and allow to cool. Cut corn from cob, and set aside.

Combine oil, vinegar, lemon juice, mustard, salt, pepper, parsley, and basil; stir well. Add corn, tomatoes, green pepper, and onion; toss lightly, and chill. Serve on lettuce, if desired. Yield: 6 servings.

Corn Relish

About 18 ears of corn
4 cups chopped cabbage
1 cup chopped sweet red pepper
1 cup chopped green pepper
1 cup chopped onion
1 tablespoon celery seeds
1 tablespoon salt
1 tablespoon turmeric
3 tablespoons mustard seeds
1 cup water
4 cups vinegar
2 cups sugar

Cook corn in boiling water 5 minutes; cut from cob, and measure 8 cups. Combine corn with remaining ingredients, and simmer 10 to 15 minutes. Bring to a boil; pack in hot, sterilized jars. Seal. Process 15 minutes in boiling-water bath. Yield: about 6 pints.

Corn Chowder

4 slices bacon
1 medium onion, chopped
2 (17-ounce) cans cream-style corn
2 cups milk
1 teaspoon salt
1/4 teaspoon pepper
1/4 cup butter or margarine

Fry bacon until crisp; remove from drippings and crumble.

Add onion to bacon drippings; cook over medium heat until transparent. Stir in corn, milk, bacon, and seasonings. Cook over medium heat until hot, stirring constantly; add butter, stirring until melted. Yield: 6 servings.

Southern Hush Puppies

2 cups cornmeal
1 tablespoon all-purpose flour
1 teaspoon soda
1 teaspoon baking powder
2 teaspoons salt
1 cup buttermilk
1 egg, slightly beaten
2 tablespoons finely chopped onion
Vegetable oil or shortening

Combine dry ingredients; add buttermilk, egg, and onion, stirring well. Carefully drop batter by tablespoonfuls into deep hot oil (370°); cook only a few at a time, turning once. Fry until hush puppies are golden brown (3 to 5 minutes). Drain well on absorbent towels. Yield: 2-1/2 dozen.

Corn Curry

1/4 cup melted margarine
3 cups frozen or canned whole kernel corn
2 tablespoons chopped green pepper
3 tablespoons chopped pimiento
3 tablespoons chopped onion
1/2 teaspoon curry powder
3/4 cup commercial sour cream
1/2 teaspoon salt
Freshly ground pepper

Combine margarine, vegetables, and curry powder in a skillet; cook over low heat 8 to 10 minutes or until vegetables are tender. Stir in sour cream, salt, and pepper. Heat thoroughly, stirring often; do not allow to boil. Yield: 6 servings.

Corn Sticks

1-1/4 cups yellow cornmeal
2/3 cup all-purpose flour
1/4 cup sugar (optional)
1 tablespoon baking powder
1/2 teaspoon salt
1 egg, beaten
1 cup milk
1/4 cup vegetable oil

Combine dry ingredients. Add egg, milk, and oil; mix lightly. Pour batter into 2 well-greased corn-stick pans. Bake at 425° for 12 to 15 minutes or until golden brown. Yield: 14 corn sticks.

Fresh Corn Pudding

2-1/2 cups fresh corn cut from cob
3 eggs, beaten
3 tablespoons finely chopped onion
1/4 cup all-purpose flour
1 teaspoon salt
1/8 teaspoon pepper
1 tablespoon sugar
Dash of ground nutmeg
2 tablespoons melted butter or margarine
2 cups milk
1/4 cup dry breadcrumbs
1/4 cup grated Parmesan cheese

Combine all ingredients except breadcrumbs and cheese, mixing well. Spoon into a lightly greased shallow 2-quart casserole. Combine breadcrumbs and cheese; sprinkle over corn mixture. Place casserole in a pan containing 1 inch hot water. Bake at 325° for 1 hour or until firm. Yield: 6 servings.

Mayan sculpture, possibly a corn god. Museum of Primitive Art

Beefy Jalapeño Cornbread

1 cup yellow cornmeal
1 cup milk
2 eggs, beaten
3/4 teaspoon salt
1/2 teaspoon soda
1/2 cup bacon drippings or vegetable oil
1 (17-ounce) can cream-style corn
1 pound ground beef
1 pound Cheddar cheese, shredded
1 onion, chopped
4 to 5 jalapeño peppers, chopped

Combine cornmeal, milk, eggs, salt, soda, bacon drippings, and corn in a mixing bowl; blend well, and set aside. Sauté ground beef until lightly browned; drain thoroughly, and set aside.

Pour half of cornmeal batter into a greased 13- x 9- x 2-inch pan; sprinkle with cheese. Crumble beef over cheese, and sprinkle with onion and peppers. Pour remaining cornmeal batter over top. Bake at 350° for 50 minutes. Yield: 10 to 12 servings.

Sour Cream Cornbread

1 cup self-rising cornmeal
2 eggs
1 (8-3/4-ounce) can cream-style corn
1 cup commercial sour cream
1/2 cup vegetable oil

Combine all ingredients, mixing well. Pour into a greased 9-inch pan; bake at 400° for 20 to 30 minutes. Yield: about 9 servings.

Scalloped Corn

1/4 cup chopped onion
2 tablespoons melted butter or margarine
2 tablespoons all-purpose flour
1 teaspoon salt
1/2 teaspoon paprika
1/4 teaspoon dry mustard
Dash of pepper
3/4 cup milk
1 (17-ounce) can whole kernel corn, drained
1 egg, beaten
1/2 cup cracker crumbs
3 tablespoons melted butter or margarine

Sauté onion in 2 tablespoons melted butter until lightly browned. Stir in flour and seasonings. Remove from heat; gradually stir in milk. Return mixture to heat; boil 1 minute, stirring constantly. Remove from heat; stir in corn and egg.

Pour mixture into a greased 1-quart baking dish. Combine crumbs and 3 tablespoons melted butter, stirring until moistened; sprinkle crumbs over casserole. Bake at 350° for 20 to 30 minutes. Yield: 4 servings.

Indian Roasted Corn

8 ears of fresh corn
3 tablespoons salt
Softened butter or margarine

Remove large outer husks from corn; turn back inner husks, and remove silk. Pull husks back over ears, and tie with heavy twine or fine wire. Dissolve salt in enough cold water to cover corn. Soak corn in salt water for 1 hour (a weight may be necessary to keep corn submerged.)

Drain corn, and place on grill over hot coals 15 to 20 minutes, turning frequently. Serve at once with butter. Yield: 8 servings.

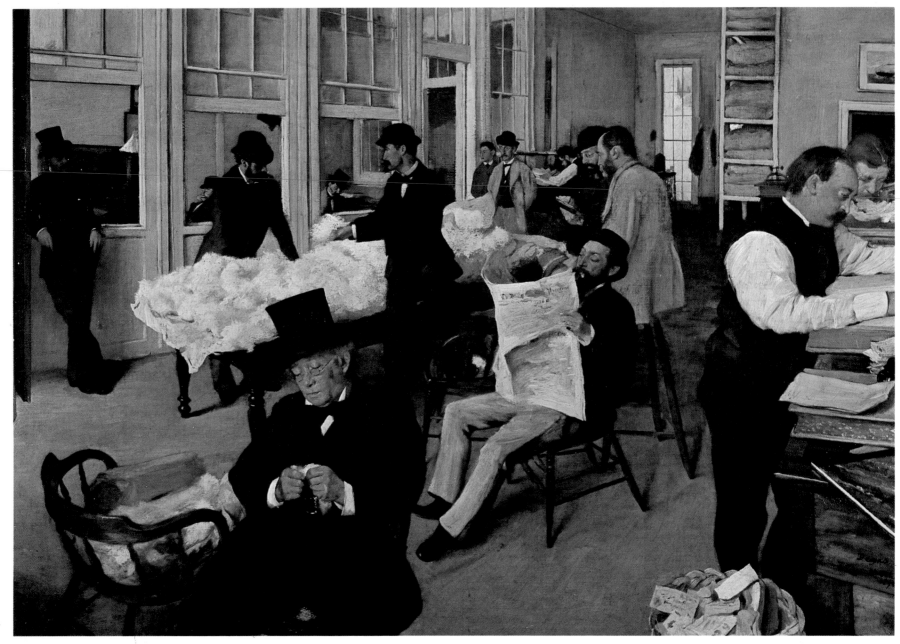

Edgar Degas: Portraits in an Office, *1872, Musée Muncipal des Beaux-Arts, Pau, France*

Creole Sampler

This Bouillabaisse a noble dish is—
A sort of soup, or broth, or stew,
A hotch-potch of all sorts of fishes
That Greenwich never could outdo;
Green herbs, red peppers, mussels, saffron,
Soles, onions, garlic, roach, and dace;
All these you can eat at Terre's tavern
In that one dish of Bouillabaisse.

The English novelist William Makepeace Thackeray—who wrote these lines about his eating experiences in New Orleans—was not the only foreigner to come under the spell of America's most exotic city. The French Impressionist painter Edgar Degas was another. New Orleans was the birthplace of Degas's mother, Celestine Musson, and the painter and his youngest brother, René, visited their mother's family in 1872. There René fell in love with and married his cousin, Estelle Musson. In *Portraits in an Office,* opposite, Edgar painted Estelle's father, Michel, a prominent New Orleans businessman, and other family members. Unlike Thackeray, Degas did not have anything to say about the famous Creole cuisine of the city— an innovative blend of French, Indian, African, and Spanish cooking that took copious advantage of the fresh fish and vegetables of the region, as in the jambalaya at right. Creole cooking is one of the few regional American cuisines totally unrelated to the English tradition of cooking. Like the city of New Orleans itself, it is at heart unique and a little out of the mainstream.

Photographed near a bayou by Taylor Lewis: Crawfish Jambalaya, Creole Stuffed Peppers, Baked Redfish, and Crawfish Etoufée.

Creole Cooking

A prominent United States Senator has written that the vaunted "American melting pot does not melt . . . it transforms." One blessed transformation, in the Louisiana territory, was that of the French, the Spanish, and the native into the Creole. Whether from melting pot or cooking pot, the resulting mix enriches us all.

Turkey and Sausage Gumbo

1 turkey carcass
1/2 cup vegetable oil
1/2 cup all-purpose flour
1-1/2 large onions, chopped
1/2 green pepper, chopped
1 stalk celery, chopped
1-1/2 pounds smoked sausage, cut into 2-1/2-inch pieces
Salt
Red and black pepper
1/4 cup chopped parsley
1/4 cup chopped green onion tops
Hot cooked rice
Gumbo filé (optional)

Use a turkey carcass with a little meat left on it; a smoked turkey is best. Cover carcass with water, and boil until meat leaves bones (about 1 hour). Reserve broth, and remove meat from carcass; discard bones.

Combine vegetable oil and flour in a large iron pot; cook over medium heat, stirring constantly, until a medium roux is formed. Add onion, green pepper, and celery; cook about 5 minutes or until tender, stirring constantly. Add sausage, turkey, and 2 to 3 quarts broth (add water to make 2 quarts, if necessary); simmer 1 hour.

Season gumbo to taste with salt and pepper. Stir in parsley and green onion; cook 10 minutes longer. Serve over rice. Thicken with gumbo filé, if desired. Yield: 8 to 10 servings.

Grillades and Grits

4 pounds (1/2-inch-thick) boneless round steak
1/2 cup bacon drippings, divided
1/2 cup all-purpose flour
2 cups chopped green onion
1 cup chopped onion
3/4 cup chopped celery
3/4 cup chopped green pepper
2 cloves garlic, minced
2 cups chopped fresh tomato
2/3 teaspoon thyme
1/2 teaspoon tarragon
1 cup water
1 cup dry red wine
1 tablespoon salt
1/2 teaspoon pepper
2 bay leaves
2 tablespoons Worcestershire sauce
1/2 teaspoon hot sauce
3 tablespoons chopped parsley
Parsley sprigs
Hot cooked grits, buttered

Remove and discard fat from steak; cut meat into serving-size pieces. Pound meat to 1/4-inch thickness using a meat mallet. Brown meat well in a Dutch oven in 1/4 cup bacon drippings; place meat on warm platter, and set aside.

Add remaining bacon drippings to Dutch oven; stir in flour. Cook over low heat, stirring constantly, until flour is dark brown. Add onion, celery, green pepper, and garlic; sauté until onion is transparent. Add tomato, thyme, and tarragon; cook over low heat 3 minutes. Stir in next 7 ingredients.

Place meat in sauce; cover and simmer 2 hours. Discard bay leaves; stir in chopped parsley. Cool several hours at room temperature, or chill overnight.

Heat grillades thoroughly before serving, adding water if needed. Garnish with parsley sprigs. Serve over grits. Yield: 8 to 10 servings.

N-YHS

Baked Redfish

2 (3-pound) redfish
Olive oil
Salt and pepper
1 cup water
1 large onion, chopped
2 cups sliced Creole tomatoes (small red tomatoes)
3 bay leaves
2 lemons, sliced
3 fresh sweet basil leaves
1/2 cup white wine
Lemon slices
3 tablespoons minced fresh parsley
Hot cooked rice

Clean redfish thoroughly, but do not remove the head. Rub fish inside and out with olive oil, salt, and pepper. Place fish in flat baking pan. Add water, onion, tomatoes, bay leaves, lemons, basil, and wine. Bake, uncovered, at 350° for 1 hour, basting every 15 minutes. Garnish with lemon slices and parsley; serve with hot cooked rice. Yield: 8 servings.

Oreilles de Cochon (Pig's Ears)

1 cup all-purpose flour
1/4 teaspoon salt
About 1/4 cup water
Vegetable oil
1 (12-ounce) can cane syrup
Finely chopped pecans

Combine flour and salt; stir in enough water to make a stiff dough. Divide dough into 12 equal parts, and roll each into a ball. Roll out balls of dough very thin on a lightly floured surface.

Pour about 2 inches of vegetable oil in a heavy saucepan; heat to 375°. Drop a pastry circle into hot oil; using a long-handled fork, immediately stick the tines in the center of the pastry and twist quickly. Hold until set (the far side of the pastry will fold over on itself, forming an "ear"); cook until golden brown on both sides, and drain well on paper towels. Repeat procedure with remaining pastry.

Pour syrup into a heavy saucepan, and bring to a boil; cook 5 to 10 minutes, stirring occasionally. Dip each "ear" in hot syrup, coating well on both sides.

Sprinkle with finely chopped nuts, and let dry on buttered waxed paper. Serve warm or at room temperature. Yield: 1 dozen.

Crawfish Jambalaya

2 cups peeled crawfish tails
1/2 cup crawfish fat (from heads of parboiled
  crawfish)
1/2 cup margarine
2 cups chopped white onion
1 cup chopped celery
1/2 cup chopped green pepper
2 cloves garlic, chopped
1 fresh ripe tomato, chopped
3 tablespoons chopped green onion
2 bay leaves
1/4 teaspoon thyme
1 teaspoon Spanish paprika
2 tablespoons chopped parsley
6 cups water
3 cups regular uncooked rice
Salt and pepper to taste
Hot sauce (optional)

Parboil crawfish, remove fat, and peel tails. Set aside.

Melt margarine in large iron pot with a cover. Add onion, celery, green pepper, and garlic; cook until vegetables are clear. Add chopped tomato, crawfish tails, and fat; cook 5 minutes. Add green onion, bay leaves, thyme, paprika, and parsley; cook 5 minutes more.

Add water, rice, salt, and pepper. Bring to a boil while stirring; cover and reduce heat to simmer. Cook for 15 minutes. Do not remove cover until rice is done. Add hot sauce, if desired. Yield: 6 to 8 servings.

Note: If crawfish are not available, 2 cups peeled and deveined shrimp may be substituted. Delete crawfish fat from recipe if shrimp is used.

Bananas Foster

6 tablespoons butter
1/2 cup firmly packed brown sugar
1/2 teaspoon ground cinnamon
4 bananas, halved lengthwise
1/2 cup banana-flavored liqueur
3/4 cup rum
1 pint vanilla ice cream

Melt butter in a chafing dish. Add sugar and cinnamon; cook syrup over medium heat until bubbly. Add bananas; heat 3 to 4 minutes, basting constantly with syrup.

Combine liqueur and rum in a small, long-handled pan; heat just until warm. Ignite with a long match, and pour over bananas. Baste bananas with sauce until flames die down. Serve immediately over ice cream. Yield: 4 servings.

Creole Stuffed Peppers

8 small to medium green peppers
2 pounds pork shoulder
1/2 pound pork liver
2 medium onions, peeled
Salt and pepper
Ground red pepper
1 cup cooked rice
Meat broth
2 cups tomato puree

Carefully remove tops, seeds, and fibers from green peppers. Place in small amount of water; parboil for 10 minutes. Remove from water very carefully with slotted spoon so that sides are not broken. Set aside.

Cook pork, liver, and onions in boiling salted water until tender; remove from liquid. Strain liquid and set aside. Put meat and onions through a food grinder. Add salt, pepper, and red pepper to taste.

Combine cooked rice, meat mixture, and enough reserved meat broth to hold mixture together. Stuff mixture into peppers. Place in a baking dish; pour tomato puree over peppers. Bake at 300° about 20 minutes. This may be served at once, or it will taste even better if reheated the next day. Yield: 8 servings.

Red Beans and Rice

1 pound dried red beans
1 large ham bone
1 large onion, chopped
1 large clove garlic, chopped
1 bay leaf
1/8 to 1/4 teaspoon red pepper
2 teaspoons salt
1 pound smoked mild or hot link sausage, cut
  into 2-inch pieces
Hot cooked rice

Sort beans, and wash thoroughly; cover with water, and soak overnight.

Drain beans, and place in a heavy saucepan; cover with water. Add ham bone, onion, garlic, bay leaf, and red pepper; bring to a boil. Reduce heat; cover and simmer 2 hours or until beans are tender. Add more water during cooking, if necessary.

Add salt and sausage to beans. Simmer, uncovered, until a thick gravy forms; stir occasionally. Serve over hot rice. Yield: 4 servings.

Pecan Pralines

2 cups sugar
1 teaspoon soda
1 cup buttermilk
1/8 teaspoon salt
2 tablespoons butter or margarine
1 tablespoon light corn syrup
2-1/2 cups pecan halves

Combine sugar, soda, buttermilk, and salt in a heavy 4-quart saucepan; cook over medium heat to 210° (about 5 minutes), stirring constantly. Add butter, syrup, and pecans; continue cooking until candy reaches 234° (soft ball stage) or about 5 minutes more, stirring constantly.

Remove from heat; beat with a wooden spoon for 2 to 3 minutes, just until mixture begins to thicken. Working rapidly, drop tablespoonfuls onto lightly buttered waxed paper; let cool. Wrap pralines in waxed paper and store in airtight container. Yield: about 18 (3-inch) pralines.

Crawfish Etouffée

1 large onion, chopped
1/2 green pepper, chopped
1/3 cup melted butter or vegetable oil
Fat from 2 pounds crawfish tails
1 tablespoon cornstarch
1 cup water
2 pounds crawfish tails
Salt and pepper to taste
Red pepper to taste
1 tablespoon chopped parsley
1 tablespoon chopped green onion
Hot cooked rice

Sauté onion and green pepper in butter until tender; add crawfish fat. Dissolve cornstarch in small amount of water; add to sautéed vegetables with remaining water; cook and stir until slightly thickened. Add crawfish tails, salt, pepper, and red pepper and simmer 10 to 15 minutes longer. Just before serving, stir in parsley and green onion. Serve over rice. Yield: about 6 servings.

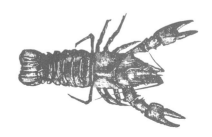

Hans Eworth: Lord Cobham and Family at Table, *1567, Marquess of Bath*

Desserts

The great families of the Old South liked to boast of their ancestral connections with the English gentry and to compare the stately pace of plantation life with that of the great country houses of England. Lord Cobham's house in Kent would have been exactly the sort of establishment they had in mind. His Lordship, opposite, poses with his heirs apparent and Lady Cobham (standing) and another imposing woman, possibly a relation. The two infants, with ruffs at their chins and wrists, appear to be twins, as do the little girls at center. The children gather around the pleasant table with their simple dessert—fresh fruit—set before them and their pets all around: a monkey, who sits boldly on his small mistress's plate, a parrot, a songbird, and a puppy. The serious-faced youngsters are dressed exactly like the adults, of whom they appear to be charming and perfectly behaved miniatures—as in some ways they were. In 1567, when this portrait was painted, children were quite literally expected to be seen and not heard. By the age of five or six, a poor man's child might be apprenticed or in service; the rich man's child, like the little Cobhams, was probably already struggling with Latin and Greek. The notion of childhood as a time for fun and play had occurred to hardly anybody, and the idea that children and rich desserts were a natural pair would certainly not have been accepted in a proper household. Happily, children are no longer laced up in corsetlike apparel, nor are babies required to appear at table in a ruff. American children are far more likely to look like the youngster at right, contemplating the geology of a banana split.

An ice cream spectacular photographed by Taylor Lewis

Desserts

"I can resist everything except temptation," said Oscar Wilde. And he has a lot of company. Desserts—particularly chocolate desserts—are the most sought-after recipes in an occasionally calorie-counting America.

Lemon Ice Cream

3 cups sugar
4 cups milk
1 cup half-and-half
2 cups whipping cream
Grated rind of 5 to 6 lemons
3/4 cup fresh lemon juice
2 egg whites, beaten
Yellow food coloring (optional)

Combine sugar, milk, half-and-half, whipping cream, and lemon rind. Pour lemon juice over milk mixture, and beat well. Fold in egg whites. Add food coloring, if desired.

Pour mixture into freezer can of a 1-gallon hand-turned or electric freezer. Freeze according to manufacturer's instructions. Let ripen at least 2 hours. Yield: 1 gallon.

Pecan Pie

1/2 cup melted butter or margarine
1 cup sugar
1 cup light corn syrup
4 eggs, beaten
1 teaspoon vanilla extract
1/4 teaspoon salt
1 unbaked 9-inch pastry shell
About 1 cup pecan halves

Combine butter, sugar, and corn syrup; cook over low heat, stirring constantly, until sugar is dissolved. Cool. Add eggs, vanilla, and salt; mix well.

Pour filling into pastry shell, and top with pecan halves. Bake at 325° for 50 to 55 minutes. Yield: one 9-inch pie.

Pecan Balls with Hot Fudge Sauce

2 cups chopped pecans
1 quart vanilla ice cream
Hot Fudge Sauce

Place pecans in a shallow baking pan; bake at 300° about 15 minutes, stirring frequently. Cool and set aside. Shape ice cream into 6 balls; roll each in pecans. Place on waxed paper-lined cookie sheet; cover and store in freezer until needed. Serve with Hot Fudge Sauce. Yield: 6 servings.

Hot Fudge Sauce:
1/2 cup butter or margarine
4 (1-ounce) squares unsweetened chocolate
3 cups sugar
1/2 teaspoon salt
1 (13-ounce) can evaporated milk

Combine butter and chocolate in top of a double boiler; cook over hot, not boiling, water until melted. Gradually stir in sugar, about 1/4 cup at a time, stirring very well after each addition (mixture will be very thick and dry). Add salt. Add evaporated milk slowly, stirring constantly. Serve hot. Yield: 4 cups.

Molasses Spice Cake

1/2 cup shortening
1/2 cup sugar
1 egg
1 cup molasses
2-1/2 cups all-purpose flour
1-1/2 teaspoons soda
1/2 teaspoon salt
1 teaspoon ground cinnamon
1 teaspoon ground ginger
1/2 teaspoon ground cloves
1 cup boiling water
1 (9-ounce) carton frozen whipped topping, thawed

Cream shortening and sugar until light and fluffy; add egg and molasses, beating well. Combine dry ingredients; add to batter alternately with water, mixing well after each addition. Pour into 2 well-greased 9-inch cake pans.

Bake at 350° for 30 to 35 minutes. Let cake cool in pans 10 minutes; remove from pans, and cool completely. Spread whipped topping between layers and on top of cake. Yield: one 9-inch layer cake.

Fudge-Sauced Ice Cream Pie

1 (13-ounce) can evaporated milk
1 (6-ounce) package semisweet chocolate morsels
1 cup miniature marshmallows
1/4 teaspoon salt
Vanilla wafers
1/2 gallon vanilla ice cream, softened and divided
Toasted slivered almonds

Combine milk, chocolate morsels, marshmallows, and salt in a saucepan; cook over low heat, stirring constantly, until the mixture is smooth and thickened (about 5 minutes). Cool to room temperature.

Line an 8-inch springform pan with vanilla wafers. Spread half of ice cream over vanilla wafers. Freeze until slightly firm. Spread half of chocolate sauce over ice cream; freeze until slightly firm. Spoon remaining ice cream over chocolate layer; freeze until slightly firm. Spread remaining chocolate sauce over ice cream, and sprinkle with almonds. Freeze several hours or until firm. Yield: about 8 servings.

Lemon Cheesecake

1-1/2 cups zwieback crumbs
1 cup sugar, divided
3/4 teaspoon ground cinnamon
6 tablespoons melted butter or margarine
1/4 cup all-purpose flour
1/4 teaspoon salt
2 (8-ounce) packages cream cheese, softened
1 teaspoon vanilla extract
2 tablespoons lemon juice
1/2 teaspoon grated lemon rind
4 eggs, separated
1 evaporated milk or whipping cream

Combine zwieback crumbs, 1/4 cup sugar, cinnamon, and butter; mix well, and press onto bottom and sides of an 8-inch springform pan.

Combine 1/2 cup sugar, flour, and salt; add cream cheese, and beat until light and fluffy. Add vanilla, lemon juice, and lemon rind. Add egg yolks, one at a time, beating well after each addition; add evaporated milk, blending well.

Beat egg whites until foamy; gradually add remaining 1/4 cup sugar, and beat until stiff. Fold egg whites into cream cheese mixture. Pour mixture into prepared crust, and bake at 325° for 1 hour and 15 minutes. Cool before removing from pan. Yield: 10 servings.

Chocolate Mousse

1 (6-ounce) package semisweet chocolate morsels
6 eggs, separated
2 teaspoons vanilla extract

Melt chocolate in top of a double boiler; remove from heat. Beat yolks, and stir in a small amount of chocolate. Gradually add yolk mixture to remaining chocolate, stirring until blended well. Cool. Stir in vanilla.

Beat egg whites until stiff peaks form; fold into chocolate mixture. Spoon into individual serving dishes. Chill at least 4 hours before serving. Yield: 8 to 10 servings.

Caribbean Fudge Pie

1/4 cup butter or margarine
3/4 cup firmly packed brown sugar
3 eggs
1 (12-ounce) package semisweet chocolate morsels, melted
2 teaspoons instant coffee powder
1 teaspoon rum extract
1/4 cup all-purpose flour
1-1/2 cups chopped pecans, divided
1 unbaked 9-inch pastry shell
Whipped cream (optional)

Cream butter and sugar; add eggs, one at a time, beating well after each addition. Add melted chocolate, coffee powder, and rum extract. Stir in flour and 1 cup pecans. Pour into pastry shell; sprinkle with remaining pecans.

Bake at 375° for 25 minutes or until done. Cool; top with whipped cream, if desired. Yield: one 9-inch pie.

Snow White Buttermilk Ice Cream

1 quart buttermilk
1 pint whipping cream
2 cups sugar
1 tablespoon vanilla extract

Combine all ingredients, stirring well. Pour into freezer can of a 1-gallon hand-turned or electric freezer. Freeze according to manufacturer's directions. Yield: 1/2 gallon.

Note: Recipe may be doubled.

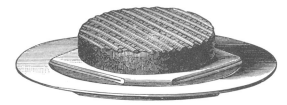

An engraving from a 19th-century Swedish cookbook.

Holiday Log Cake

3/4 teaspoon baking powder
1/4 teaspoon salt
4 eggs, at room temperature
3/4 cup sugar
3/4 cup all-purpose flour
1/4 cup cocoa
1 teaspoon vanilla extract
2 to 3 tablespoons powdered sugar
2 cups sweetened whipped cream
3 (1-ounce) squares unsweetened chocolate
1/4 cup butter or margarine
1 tablespoon instant coffee granules
Dash of salt
1/3 cup boiling water
About 2-1/2 cups sifted powdered sugar
Candied cherries

Grease a 15- x 10- x 1-inch pan; line with waxed paper and grease lightly. Set aside.

Combine baking powder, 1/4 teaspoon salt, and eggs in mixing bowl; beat at medium speed of electric mixer. Add sugar gradually, beating until thick and light colored. Fold in flour, cocoa, and vanilla.

Spread mixture evenly into prepared pan. Bake at 400° for 13 minutes or until surface springs back when gently pressed.

Sift 2 to 3 tablespoons powdered sugar in a 15- x 10-inch rectangle on a linen towel. Turn cake out on sugar; remove waxed paper from cake. Trim crisp edges, if necessary. Starting with the short end, carefully roll cake and towel, jellyroll fashion. Cool thoroughly on wire rack. Unroll; spread with whipped cream, and reroll. Chill.

Melt chocolate in top of a double boiler; blend in butter, coffee, salt, and boiling water, stirring until smooth. Cool to lukewarm. Stir in about 2-1/2 cups powdered sugar to make a spreading consistency. Spread frosting evenly over cake. Mark with tines of a fork to resemble bark of a tree. Decorate with candied cherries. Refrigerate until serving time. Yield: 8 to 10 servings.

Deep-Dish Apple Pie

8 cooking apples, peeled and thinly sliced
1-1/4 cups sugar
3 tablespoons all-purpose flour
1-1/2 teaspoons ground cinnamon
1/4 teaspoon ground nutmeg
1/8 teaspoon salt
3 tablespoons butter or margarine
Pastry (recipe follows)

Arrange apple slices in a lightly greased 9-inch baking dish. Combine sugar, flour, cinnamon, nutmeg, and salt; sprinkle over apples, and dot with butter. Top with pastry, and bake at 400° for 40 minutes or until golden brown. Yield: 6 to 8 servings.

Pastry:
1-1/4 cups all-purpose flour
1/4 teaspoon salt
2 tablespoons shortening
4 tablespoons cold butter or margarine
3 to 4 tablespoons cold water

Combine flour and salt; cut in shortening. Cut butter into small pieces, and add to flour mixture; cut in until mixture resembles coarse cornmeal. Stir in only enough water to moisten flour; form dough into a ball. Wrap in plastic wrap, and chill 30 minutes.

Roll dough to 1/4-inch thickness on a lightly floured surface, and cut into 1-inch-wide strips. Arrange lattice fashion over filling. Yield: pastry for one 9-inch pie.

Carrot Cake

4 eggs, beaten
1-1/4 cups vegetable oil
2 cups grated raw carrots
3 cups all-purpose flour
3 teaspoons baking powder
2 teaspoons soda
2 teaspoons ground cinnamon
1/2 teaspoon salt
2 cups sugar
1/2 cup chopped pecans

Combine eggs and oil, mixing well; stir in carrots; and set aside. Sift dry ingredients three times. Add to carrot mixture gradually, mixing well. Stir in pecans.

Pour batter into a greased 10-inch tube pan. Bake at 350° for 65 to 75 minutes. Yield: one 10-inch cake.

Horace Pippin: Cabin in the Cotton III, *1944, Collection of Roy Neuberger, New York*

For Body and Soul

Soul food is not a definable category of cuisine, being less a kind of food than an attitude toward it. "Soul" can be found anywhere, though its American home is undoubtedly the South and the raw materials of soul food are corn, chicken, pork, fish, wild game, vegetables, and fruit. It was invented in the slave quarters of planatations and kept alive in cabins like the one opposite, painted by Horace Pippin in 1944. But as it evolved it became much more than slave food; indeed, its methods and its philosophy have long been the soul of old-fashioned Southern cooking. For while soul cooking is poor people's cooking, it was shaped as much by ingenuity as by poverty. The soul cook despises nothing except laziness in the kitchen and throws out nothing edible, looking upon even the tops of turnips and the entrails of hogs as a pleasant culinary challenge. She or he is capable of dealing with a plentiful harvest as well. Some of the dishes in this section, such as sweet-potato pie and peach dumplings, contain such luxuries as honey and cream and spices. But if a soul cook has nothing but cornmeal, bacon drippings, dried peas, and an onion, she can make a good meal of that, too.

Slave-cabin cooking, contrary to popular belief, was not devised merely from big-house handouts. More often, slaves raised and hunted their own food. Frederick Law Olmsted, traveling through the South in the 1850s (he later became famous as the designer of New York's Central Park), claimed that the whites, rich and poor alike, often subsisted on pork, cornbread, and sorghum; the slaves, however, raised and ate vegetables— particularly sweet potatoes—and were sometimes healthier and better nourished than their masters.

From the bottom, we have Fried Ham with Red-Eye Gravy, Black-Eyed Peas, Fresh Greens, Cornbread, and Sweet Potato Pie. Photo by Taylor Lewis.

Soul Food

Soul food pays less heed to the disembodied hereafter than to the very corporeal now—for everyone's culinary pleasure.

Old-Fashioned Sweet Potato Pie

2 cups cooked, mashed sweet potatoes
1 cup firmly packed brown sugar
1/2 cup butter or margarine, softened
2 eggs, separated
1/2 teaspoon ground ginger
1/2 teaspoon ground cinnamon
1/2 teaspoon ground nutmeg
1/4 teaspoon salt
1/2 cup evaporated milk
1/4 cup sugar
1 unbaked 10-inch pastry shell
Whipped topping (optional)

Combine sweet potatoes, brown sugar, butter, egg yolks, spices, and salt in a large mixing bowl; beat until light and fluffy. Add evaporated milk; mix just until combined.

Beat egg whites until foamy; gradually add sugar, beating until stiff. Fold into potato mixture. Pour filling into pastry shell. Bake at 400° for 10 minutes; reduce heat to 350°, and bake an additional 45 to 50 minutes or until set. Cool. Top with whipped topping, if desired. Yield: one 10-inch pie.

Fried Okra

1 to 1-1/4 pounds okra
8 cups water
1/2 cup salt
Cornmeal
Vegetable oil

Wash okra well; drain. Cut off tip and stem ends; cut okra crosswise into 1/2-inch slices.

Combine water and salt; pour over okra. Soak 30 minutes; drain, rinse well, and drain again. Roll okra in cornmeal, and fry in hot oil until golden brown. Drain on absorbent towels. Yield: 6 servings.

Hopping John

2 cups dried black-eyed peas
2 quarts water
4 slices bacon, chopped
1 small onion, chopped
1 cup uncooked regular rice
1-1/2 teaspoons salt
1/4 teaspoon pepper
2 cups water

Sort peas, and wash thoroughly. Place in a heavy saucepan or Dutch oven; cover with water. Bring to a boil, and boil 2 minutes. Cover and let soak overnight. Drain and rinse well. Combine peas and 2 quarts water; bring to a boil. Cover and reduce heat to low; cook until tender.

Fry bacon until crisp; drain on absorbent towels, and set aside. Set aside 2 tablespoons bacon drippings. Sauté onion in remaining drippings until tender; drain on absorbent towels.

Add onion, 2 tablespoons bacon drippings, rice, salt, pepper, and 2 cups water to peas. Cover and cook over low heat 1 hour or until rice is tender; stir occasionally and add water, if needed. Sprinkle with the cooked bacon before serving. Yield: about 6 to 8 servings.

Sweet Potato Pudding

2 pounds sweet potatoes, cooked and peeled
1/4 cup melted butter or margarine
6 tablespoons brown sugar
3 tablespoons dark rum
1/2 teaspoon salt
Chopped pecans

Combine potatoes, butter, sugar, rum, and salt; beat until smooth. Spoon into a lightly greased 2-quart casserole; sprinkle with pecans. Bake at 350° for 30 minutes. Yield: 6 servings.

Fried Ham with Red-Eye Gravy

Slice ham about 1/4 inch thick. Cut gashes in fat to keep ham from curling. Place slices in a heavy skillet and cook slowly. Turn several times, and cook until ham is brown. Remove from pan and keep warm. To the drippings in the skillet, add about 1/2 cup hot water for every pound of ham; cook until gravy turns red. A little strong coffee may be added to deepen the color. Serve hot with fried ham and hot biscuits.

Dixie Fried Chicken

1 (2- to 3-pound) broiler-fryer chicken, cut up
Salt and pepper
2 cups all-purpose flour
1 teaspoon red pepper
1 egg, slightly beaten
1/2 cup milk
Hot oil

Season chicken with salt and pepper. Combine flour and red pepper; set aside. Combine egg and milk; dip chicken in egg mixture; then dredge in flour mixture, coating well.

Heat 1 inch of oil in a skillet; place chicken in skillet. Cover and cook over medium heat about 30 minutes or until golden brown; turn occasionally. Drain on paper towels. Yield: 4 servings.

Cracklin' Cornbread

1 cup self-rising cornmeal
1/3 cup self-rising flour
1 tablespoon sugar
1 teaspoon pepper
3 eggs, beaten
1 cup buttermilk
1/3 cup milk
1 tablespoon melted shortening
1 cup cracklings

Combine dry ingredients. Add eggs, buttermilk, and milk; stir well. Add shortening and cracklings; stir well. Pour batter into a hot, greased 9-inch cast-iron skillet. Bake at 350° for 45 to 50 minutes or until golden brown. Yield: 6 to 8 servings.

Fresh Greens

1 large bunch greens (about 2 to 2-1/2 pounds)
1/4 pound salt pork, diced
About 3-1/2 cups boiling water
Salt to taste

Check leaves of fresh greens carefully; remove pulpy stems and discolored spots on leaves. Wash thoroughly in several changes of warm water; add a little salt to the last water. Drain in colander.

Cook diced salt pork about 10 minutes in boiling water in covered saucepan. Add washed greens a few at a time; cover pot, and cook slowly for about 1 hour or until greens are tender. Do not overcook. Add additional salt, if needed. Yield: about 6 servings.

Spoonbread

1 cup cornmeal
3 cups milk, divided
1 teaspoon salt
1 teaspoon baking powder
2 tablespoons vegetable oil
3 eggs, separated

Combine cornmeal and 2 cups milk in a saucepan; cook over medium heat, stirring constantly, until consistency of mush. Remove from heat; add salt, baking powder, oil, and 1 cup milk.

Beat egg yolks, and stir into cornmeal mixture; fold in stiffly beaten egg whites. Pour into a 1-1/2-quart casserole. Bake at 325° for 1 hour. Yield: 6 servings.

Fried Green Tomatoes

3 large, firm green tomatoes
Salt and pepper to taste
1/2 cup cornmeal
Bacon drippings or shortening

Cut tomatoes into 1/4-inch slices. Season with salt and pepper; dredge in cornmeal. Heat bacon drippings in a heavy skillet; add tomatoes, and fry slowly until browned, turning once. Yield: 4 servings.

Turnip Greens with Bacon

1 pound slab bacon
3 quarts water
2-1/2 pounds turnip greens
1 clove garlic
1 small pod hot pepper
1-1/2 teaspoons salt
Salt

Rinse meat; place in a Dutch oven, and add water. Bring to a boil; reduce heat.

Check leaves of greens carefully; remove and discard pulpy stems and discolored leaves. Wash leaves thoroughly to remove grit. Add greens, a few at a time, to bacon and water.

Bring to a boil; cover, and lower heat. Simmer 30 minutes; remove cover, and add garlic, pepper, and salt. Cover, and cook over low heat 45 minutes. Remove cover, and cook 15 minutes.

Remove greens from liquid with a slotted spoon; place in a shallow bowl, discarding garlic. Remove bacon; slice, and serve with greens. Add salt to taste. Yield: 6 servings.

Okra and Tomatoes

1 pound fresh okra
1/4 cup bacon drippings
1 onion, chopped
1 green pepper, chopped
12 peeled fresh tomatoes or 1 (28-ounce) can whole tomatoes, drained
1 teaspoon sugar
1 teaspoon salt
1/2 teaspoon pepper
1 lemon, cut in wedges
1 tablespoon all-purpose flour
1 tablespoon water

Cover okra with water, and cook until tender; drain. Heat bacon drippings in a saucepan; add onion and green pepper, and sauté until tender. Add tomatoes, sugar, salt, pepper, lemon, and okra. Cover and simmer 15 minutes.

Combine flour and 1 tablespoon water, blending until smooth; add to okra and tomatoes. Cook until thickened, stirring constantly. Remove lemon wedges before serving. Yield: 4 servings.

Country Peach Dumplings

1-1/2 cups all-purpose flour
2 teaspoons baking powder
1/2 teaspoon salt
5 tablespoons shortening
1/2 cup milk
6 large, ripe peaches, peeled and pitted
3/4 cup plus 2 tablespoons sugar
Ground nutmeg
2 tablespoons honey
Milk
2 tablespoons melted butter

Combine flour, baking powder, and salt; cut in shortening with 2 knives or a pastry blender until mixture resembles coarse cornmeal. Add 1/2 cup milk, mixing well.

Roll dough to 1/8-inch thickness on a lightly floured surface; cut into six 7-inch squares.

Place a peach in center of each square; top each with 2 tablespoons sugar, dash of nutmeg, and 1 teaspoon honey. Moisten edges of dough with milk; pull corners of square over peach. Pinch dough together, sealing all seams.

Place in a lightly greased 13- x 9- x 2-inch baking dish. Drizzle each dumpling with 1 teaspoon butter; sprinkle all with remaining 2 tablespoons sugar. Bake at 400° for 35 to 40 minutes. Yield: 6 servings.

Garlic Baked Grits

1 cup uncooked grits
4 cups water
2 eggs, slightly beaten
1/2 cup butter or margarine
1 (6-ounce) roll pasteurized process cheese food with garlic, cubed
Dash of garlic salt

Cook grits in water according to package directions. Stir small amount of hot grits into eggs; add egg mixture to remainder of grits. Stir in butter, cheese, and garlic salt. Spoon mixture into a greased 2-quart casserole. Bake at 350° for 1 hour. Yield: 6 to 8 servings.

Black-Eyed Peas

1 pound dry black-eyed peas
5 to 6 cups water
1 small ham hock
1 to 3 teaspoons salt
1 large whole onion

Put dry peas in colander in sink of cold water, or wash under cold running water; wash well and remove faulty peas. Drain and place in heavy 6- to 8-quart kettle. Cover and soak 12 hours or overnight.

The next day, add ham hock to kettle (add more water if water does not cover peas) and bring to a boil. Reduce heat and add 1 teaspoon or more salt (it is better to start with a smaller amount if salty ham hock is used). Add whole onion. Cover kettle and simmer about 1 hour or until peas are tender. To avoid excessive breaking of peas, do not stir during cooking. Add more salt if needed. Yield: 6 (3/4 cup) servings.

May Follows, 1971, by Raymond Hunt. The Newark Museum

59

Peter Carl Fabergé: Renaissance Egg, 1894, *Forbes Magazine Collection*

What the Hen Doth Lay

The hen," observed the English novelist Samuel Butler, "is the egg's way of producing another egg." The egg opposite was Peter Carl Fabergé's way of showing what a consummate craftsman could produce. This exquisite object, eight inches long, is made of milky agate set with diamonds and rubies. The date on the top of the egg—1894—is also fashioned of diamonds and rubies. Fabergé was a goldsmith of French descent who worked in Imperial Russia in the last century. His clients were chiefly regal and ducal—who else could have afforded him? His eggs were most often designed as Easter presents, for in the Russian Orthodox Church Easter is the time for gifts. This egg and a number of others, equally extravagant, were the gifts of Czar Alexander III to Czarina Maria Fëdorovna. Alexander was the last Romanov to serve out his term in peace. His son and successor, Nicholas II (also a Fabergé customer), was shot by revolutionaries at Ekaterinburg in 1918, together with his wife Alexandra and all their children. The era of the diamond–studded Easter egg, at least in Russia, came thus to its terrible end.

It is no wonder that Fabergé found the egg an inspiring shape. An eggshell is the perfect example of package design, with or without encrustations of diamonds. From the chick's point of view, it offers protection, is precisely the right size, and is relatively easy to get out of when the time comes. It is equally perfect from the cook's point of view. It keeps the egg clean, is discardable and biodegradable and can serve as a cooking utensil for the egg or an ideal tool for separating the white from the yolk. The omelet at right is one guise the egg can take when removed from its shell.

Golden Filled Omelet photographed by Charles Beck

Eggs

No matter which came first, once the egg had definitely appeared, it became the central ingredient in an extensive sub-cuisine ranging from the basic boiled to the sophisticated soufflé. Two classics included here are New Orleans-style Eggs Benedict and Eggs Hussarde.

Shirred Eggs

4 eggs
Dash of salt
Dash of pepper
1/4 cup half-and-half
Shredded sharp cheese (optional)

Break 1 egg into each of 4 buttered 6-ounce custard cups. Sprinkle with salt and pepper; add 1 tablespoon half-and-half. Set cups in a 9- x 9- x 1-3/4-inch baking pan.

Pour hot water into pan to a depth of 1 inch. Bake at 325° for 10 to 15 minutes or until eggs are firm. If desired, top each egg with cheese after baking; return to oven, and bake 5 to 10 minutes longer. Yield: 4 servings.

Shrimp-Crab Stuffed Eggs

1-1/2 dozen hard-cooked eggs
1 (6-ounce) package frozen shrimp and crabmeat, thawed and drained
2/3 cup mayonnaise or salad dressing
1 tablespoon chili sauce
1 tablespoon grated onion
1 teaspoon finely chopped green pepper
1 teaspoon chopped pimiento
Parsley
Pitted ripe olives, quartered

Cut eggs in half; remove yolks, and place in small mixing bowl. Mash egg yolks, and blend in next 6 ingredients; stuff egg whites with yolk mixture. Garnish with parsley and ripe olives. Yield: 3 dozen.

Golden Filled Omelet

2 eggs
1/4 teaspoon salt
Dash of pepper
1 tablespoon water
About 1 tablespoon butter or margarine
2 tablespoons sautéed mushroom slices
2 tablespoons shredded cheese

Gently blend first 4 ingredients. Melt butter in an 8- or 10-inch omelet pan or skillet; heat until just hot enough to sizzle a drop of water. Pour egg mixture into pan.

Lift edge of omelet with a spatula and tilt pan to allow uncooked egg mixture to run underneath. When mixture is set, sprinkle mushroom and cheese on half of omelet. Fold omelet in half and place on a warm plate. Yield: 1 serving.

Cheesy Mexican Omelet

4 eggs, well beaten
2 tablespoons milk
1/2 cup picante sauce, divided
1/8 teaspoon salt
1/8 teaspoon pepper
1 tablespoon butter or margarine
1 to 1-1/2 cups shredded sharp Cheddar cheese

Combine eggs, milk, 2 tablespoons picante sauce, salt, and pepper; mix well. Melt butter in an 8- or 10-inch omelet pan or skillet; heat until just hot enough to sizzle a drop of water. Pour in egg mixture all at once.

As mixture starts to cook, gently lift edges of omelet with a fork and tilt pan to allow uncooked egg mixture to run underneath.

When mixture is set and no longer runs, sprinkle cheese on half of omelet; cover pan. Remove pan from heat and let stand 1 to 2 minutes or until cheese melts and eggs are firm on top.

Fold omelet in half, and place on a warm platter. Top with remaining picante sauce. Yield: 2 to 3 servings.

Breakfast Soufflé

1-1/2 pounds bulk pork sausage
9 eggs, beaten
3 cups milk
1-1/2 teaspoons dry mustard
1 teaspoon salt
3 slices bread, cut into 1/4-inch cubes
1-1/2 cups shredded Cheddar cheese

Cook sausage over medium heat until done, stirring to crumble. Drain well on paper towels; set aside.

Combine sausage and remaining ingredients, mixing well. Pour into a well-greased 13- x 9- x 2-inch baking pan. Refrigerate, covered, overnight. Bake at 350° for 1 hour. Yield: 8 to 10 servings.

Smoked Egg Dip

12 hard-cooked eggs, finely chopped
2 tablespoons butter or margarine, softened
1-1/2 teaspoons liquid smoke
1 tablespoon lemon juice or vinegar
2 teaspoons prepared mustard
2 teaspoons Worcestershire sauce
8 drops hot sauce
1-1/4 teaspoons salt
1/2 teaspoon pepper
1 cup mayonnaise or salad dressing
3 thinly sliced radishes

Combine all ingredients except radishes; beat at medium speed of electric mixer until smooth. Chill at least 1 hour; beat until fluffy.

Garnish with radish slices; serve with vegetables, crackers, or chips. Yield: about 4 cups.

Baked Egg Custard

3 eggs, slightly beaten
1/2 cup sugar
1/4 teaspoon salt
2 cups scalded milk
1 teaspoon vanilla extract
Ground nutmeg

Combine eggs, sugar, and salt. Slowly add milk and vanilla, blending well. Pour mixture into a 1-quart casserole or individual custard cups; sprinkle with nutmeg.

Place casserole or cups in a shallow pan with a small amount of water. Bake at 325° for 30 to 40 minutes or until knife inserted halfway between center and edge comes out clean. Serve warm or chilled. Yield: 4 servings.

Swiss Egg Bake

1 cup chopped onion
1 tablespoon butter or margarine
8 hard-cooked eggs, sliced
2 cups shredded Swiss cheese
1 (10-3/4-ounce) can cream of mushroom soup,
  undiluted
3/4 cup milk
1 teaspoon prepared mustard
1/2 teaspoon seasoned salt
1/4 teaspoon pepper
1/4 teaspoon dillweed
6 slices rye bread

Sauté onion in butter until tender; sprinkle in an 11-1/2- x 7-1/2- x 1-1/2-inch dish. Arrange egg slices over onion; sprinkle with cheese.

Combine soup and remaining ingredients except bread; blend well. Pour over cheese. Cut bread into triangles, and arrange on top of soup mixture. Bake at 350° for 40 minutes. Place under broiler 1 minute. Yield: about 6 servings.

Pickled Eggs

2 teaspoons ground ginger
2 teaspoons pickling spice
12 peppercorns
2 cups malt vinegar
12 hard-cooked eggs, peeled
2 medium onions, sliced
3 cloves garlic
1/2 teaspoon dillweed

Combine ginger, pickling spice, peppercorns, and vinegar in a medium saucepan. Bring to a boil; reduce heat, and simmer 5 minutes.

Place eggs in a crock or glass jar. Pour hot liquid over eggs to cover; add water if necessary to cover. Add onion, garlic, and dillweed.

Cover, and refrigerate at least 4 days. Eggs may be kept in pickling liquid several months. Serve in wedges with salt and pepper to taste. Yield: 12 to 24 servings.

Egg Salad

4 hard-cooked eggs, chopped
2 tablespoons prepared mustard
2 tablespoons mayonnaise
1/4 teaspoon salt
1/4 cup diced celery

Combine all ingredients, mixing well. Keep refrigerated until ready to use. Yield: spread for 4 to 6 sandwiches.

Detail, Still Life *by W. Bailey. Schoelkopf Gallery, N.Y.*

Eggs Hussarde

8 thin slices ham
8 thick slices tomato
8 Holland rusks
1 cup marchand de vin sauce (recipe follows)
8 soft-poached eggs
3 cups hollandaise sauce (recipe follows)
Paprika (optional)

Grill ham and tomato slices until lightly browned. Place 1 ham slice on each Holland rusk, and spoon 2 tablespoons marchand de vin sauce over each. Top with a tomato slice, an egg, and 6 tablespoons hollandaise sauce. Sprinkle with paprika, if desired. Yield: 4 servings.

Marchand de Vin Sauce:
3 tablespoons finely chopped mushrooms
1/4 cup minced ham
3 tablespoons finely chopped shallots
1/4 cup finely chopped onion
1 tablespoon minced garlic
6 tablespoons butter, melted
1 tablespoon all-purpose flour
1/4 teaspoon salt
Dash of pepper
Pinch of cayenne
1/4 cup plus 2 tablespoons beef stock
1/4 cup red wine

Sauté mushrooms, ham, shallots, onion, and garlic in butter until lightly browned. Add flour, salt, pepper, and cayenne; cook, stirring constantly, 7 to 10 minutes or until browned. Stir in beef stock and wine; simmer over low heat 35 to 45 minutes, stirring occasionally. Yield: 1 cup.

Hollandaise Sauce:
12 egg yolks
6 tablespoons lemon juice
3 cups butter, melted
3/4 teaspoon salt

Beat egg yolks in top of double boiler; stir in lemon juice. Place over hot (not boiling) water. Add butter, a little at a time, stirring constantly with a wooden spoon. Add salt. Continue cooking slowly until thickened. Yield: about 3 cups.

Eggs Benedict

2 English muffins
Butter or margarine, softened
4 slices Canadian bacon, cooked
4 soft-poached eggs
Hollandaise sauce (recipe follows)
Parsley

Separate muffins into halves; spread cut sides with butter. Broil until lightly browned.

Place a slice of Canadian bacon on each muffin half; top with poached egg, and cover with hollandaise sauce. Top each with a sprig of parsley. Yield: 2 servings.

Hollandaise Sauce:
4 egg yolks
2 tablespoons lemon juice
1 cup melted butter
1/4 teaspoon salt
1/8 teaspoon white pepper

Beat egg yolks in top of double boiler; stir in lemon juice. Place over hot (not boiling) water. Add butter a little at a time, stirring constantly with a wooden spoon. Add salt and pepper. Continue cooking slowly until thickened. Yield: about 1-1/2 cups.

Creole Eggs

8 tablespoons butter or margarine, divided
3 tablespoons all-purpose flour
1 cup milk
1 cup chopped celery
1 cup chopped onion
1 cup chopped green pepper
1 (28-ounce) can tomatoes
1 teaspoon salt
1/4 teaspoon pepper
6 hard-cooked eggs, sliced
Buttered breadcrumbs

Melt 3 tablespoons butter in a saucepan; gradually add flour, stirring constantly. Gradually add milk; cook, stirring constantly, until thick.

Melt 5 tablespoons butter in a skillet; sauté celery, onion, and green pepper until tender. Add tomatoes, salt, and pepper; cook over medium heat until thick. Add to white sauce, mixing well.

Place a layer of egg slices in a lightly greased 2-quart casserole; pour half of creamed mixture over eggs. Repeat layers. Sprinkle with breadcrumbs. Bake at 350° for 20 to 30 minutes. Yield: 6 to 8 servings.

Frans Hals: **Merrymakers at Shrovetide,** *c. 1615, Metropolitan Museum of Art*

Cheers! Prosit! Santé!

Mark Twain once remarked that water, taken in moderation, could not harm anybody—a little joke that Frans Hals might well have enjoyed. One of the most accomplished painters of seventeenth-century Holland (a time and place that witnessed an extraordinary flowering of artistic genius), Hals often set up shop among the bon vivants of Haarlem, the town where he spent most of his life. Legend later cast him as the town drunk, but if he was, he managed to remain a solid citizen and a painter well into his eighties. *Merry Makers at Shrovetide*, opposite, is a fine example of Halsian worldliness. The painter's skill is dazzling: there is not a picot on the lace ruff or a glint of light on any surface that he fails to catch. He relishes every detail. The four drinking companions, on the eve of Lent (and probably of hangover), shine with life. One thing we can surely envy them—they lived in an age that had not learned to count calories. Their too too solid flesh is not about to melt, particularly not on the meal of beer, sausages, and bread that is set before them. Well-clad burghers that they are, straightforwardly portrayed, in Hals's hands they also become a kind of emblem of good times. Good things to drink and ways to celebrate came to America early, along with the Dutch, the Scotch, the Irish, the English, and the French. And to the repertory of fermented and distilled liquids that the immigrants brought, Americans added a new liquor, bourbon, made from the New World's native corn. The trayful of drinks at right evokes this very human, very Halsian drinking heritage.

A zesty Bloody Mary, an Orange-Champagne Cocktail, and a Pep Shake photographed by Charles Beck

65

Drinks

Whether it be a formal "Ladies and Gentlemen, may I propose a toast" or a simpler "Cheers," the raising of a glass has traditionally been the symbol of occasion. Hospitality, from the fabled Southern variety to less developed forms, is usually proffered in potable form.

Zesty Bloody Mary

1-1/4 cups vodka
2-1/4 cups tomato juice
1/2 to 1 teaspoon hot sauce
1/2 teaspoon monosodium glutamate
3/4 teaspoon celery salt
1/4 teaspoon garlic powder
1-1/2 teaspoons Worcestershire sauce
Juice of 3 limes or lemons
6 stalks celery
Combine all ingredients except celery in a pitcher, mixing well. Serve over ice cubes in tall glasses; garnish with celery stalk. Yield: 6 servings.

Hot Buttered Rum

1 pound butter, softened
1 (16-ounce) package light brown sugar
1 (16-ounce) package powdered sugar
2 teaspoons ground cinnamon
2 teaspoons ground nutmeg
1 quart vanilla ice cream, softened
Light rum
Whipped cream
Cinnamon sticks
Combine butter, sugar, and spices; beat until light and fluffy. Add ice cream, stirring until well blended. Spoon mixture into a 2-quart freezer container; freeze.
To serve, thaw slightly. Place 3 tablespoons butter mixture and 1 jigger rum in a large mug; fill with boiling water. Stir well. (Any unused butter mixture can be refrozen.) Top with whipped cream, and serve with cinnamon stick stirrers. Yield: about 25 cups.

Coffee Punch

1 pint milk
2 quarts strong coffee, cooled
2 teaspoons vanilla extract
1/2 cup sugar
1 quart vanilla ice cream, softened
1/2 pint whipping cream, whipped
Ground nutmeg
Combine milk, coffee, vanilla, and sugar; blend well. Place ice cream in a punch bowl; pour in coffee mixture. Top with whipped cream and nutmeg. Yield: about 3-1/2 quarts.

Mint Tea

2 quarts boiling water
10 individual-size tea bags
1-1/2 to 2-1/2 cups sugar
Fresh mint sprigs
Juice and rind of 1-1/2 lemons
Combine water, tea bags, sugar, 10 mint sprigs, and juice and rind of lemons; cover and steep 30 minutes to 1 hour. Strain and cool. Serve over ice. Garnish each glass with a sprig of mint, if desired. Yield: 2 quarts.

Superb Brandy Alexander

1/2 gallon vanilla ice cream
1/2 cup brandy
1/4 cup crème de cacao
Combine all ingredients in container of electric blender; blend well. Yield: about 1 quart.

Milk Punch

1 (4/5-quart) bottle bourbon
3 quarts half-and-half
1/4 cup vanilla extract
Simple syrup (recipe follows)
Ground nutmeg
Combine bourbon, half-and-half, and vanilla in a 1-gallon container; add simple syrup to desired sweetness. Chill thoroughly. Sprinkle with nutmeg before serving. Yield: 1 gallon.

Simple Syrup:
1 cup sugar
1 cup water
Combine sugar and water in a small saucepan; boil 5 minutes. Cool completely before using. Yield: 1-1/4 cups.

Mint Julep

About 25 sprigs fresh mint
1 cup sugar
1-3/4 cups water
2 quarts bourbon
Bruise 15 mint sprigs well (bruise by rubbing between palms of hands). Combine bruised mint, sugar, water, and bourbon in a crock or glass container; stir to dissolve sugar. Cover and let stand 4 to 6 hours.
Remove mint from bourbon mixture. Fill glasses with shaved ice; add bourbon mixture. Garnish each drink with a mint sprig. Serve with straws. Yield: about 20 (4-ounce) juleps.

Quick Sangria

2 (6-ounce) cans frozen pink lemonade
    concentrate, thawed and undiluted
4-1/2 cups rosé, chilled
Juice of 1 lime
2 cups club soda, chilled
1 lemon, thinly sliced
1 orange, thinly sliced
Combine lemonade, rosé, and lime juice; stir until well blended. Slowly stir in soda. Garnish with lemon and orange slices. Yield: 6 to 8 servings.

Orange Breakfast Drink

1/3 cup frozen orange juice concentrate, thawed
    and undiluted
1/2 cup milk
1/2 cup water
1/4 cup sugar
1/2 teaspoon vanilla extract
5 to 6 ice cubes
Combine all ingredients in container of electric blender, and process mixture until frothy. Serve immediately. Yield: 2 servings.

Orange-Champagne Cocktail

3-1/2 cups champagne, chilled
1 (28-ounce) bottle ginger ale, chilled
2 cups orange juice, chilled
Combine champagne, ginger ale, and orange juice in a pitcher or punch bowl; stir gently. Garnish each serving with fresh fruits, if desired. Yield: 9 cups.

Wassail

4 cups pineapple juice
1-1/2 cups apricot nectar
4 cups apple cider
1 cup orange juice
2 sticks cinnamon
2 teaspoons whole cloves
1 teaspoon ground nutmeg
Bourbon to taste (optional)

Combine juices in a large saucepan. Tie spices in a cheesecloth bag; add to juice. Simmer mixture over medium heat 30 minutes; remove spice bag. Add bourbon, if desired. Serve hot. Yield: 2-1/2 quarts.

Strawberry Frappé

2 (10-ounce) packages frozen strawberries, unthawed
2 cups vodka
3 cups finely crushed ice

Combine 1 package strawberries, 1 cup vodka, and 1-1/2 cups ice in container of electric blender. Blend until no ice chunks remain. Repeat process with remaining ingredients. Serve the frappé immediately in stemmed glasses. Yield: 6 servings.

Patio Cooler

1 cup sugar
1 cup water
2 cups strong tea
2 cups pineapple juice
4 cups orange juice
1 (28-ounce) bottle ginger ale, chilled
Orange slices or wedges

Combine sugar and water in a saucepan; place over low heat until sugar is dissolved; cool.

Combine sugar mixture, tea, and fruit juices; chill several hours. Just before serving, stir in ginger ale. Garnish with orange slices. Yield: 3 quarts.

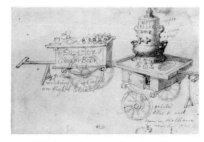

Drink-vendor carts, London, 1842

Summertime Iced Tea

6 tea bags
1 quart boiling water
1-1/2 cups sugar
1 (6-ounce) can frozen orange juice or limeade concentrate, thawed and undiluted
1 (6-ounce) can frozen lemonade concentrate, thawed and undiluted
2-1/2 quarts water

Steep tea bags in boiling water about 5 minutes; discard tea bags. Add remaining ingredients. Serve over ice. Yield: 1 gallon.

Pep Shake

1 (16-ounce) can sliced peaches, undrained
1 cup vanilla ice cream
2 eggs
Fresh mint sprigs (optional)

Combine all ingredients except mint sprigs in container of electric blender; blend until smooth. Garnish each glass with a sprig of mint, if desired. Yield: 3-1/4 cups.

Southern Egg Nog

8 eggs, separated
2-1/2 cups sugar
1 pint bourbon
5 cups whipping cream, whipped
2 cups milk
2 ounces rum
Ground nutmeg

Combine egg yolks and sugar; beat until smooth. Add bourbon very slowly, beating constantly.

Add 1 cup whipped cream to egg yolk mixture, and beat until smooth; add milk, beating well. Add remaining whipped cream, and beat until smooth; stir in rum. Fold in stiffly beaten egg whites. Chill thoroughly. Sprinkle with nutmeg before serving. Yield: about 14 cups.

Kahlúa Velvet Frosty

1 cup Kahlúa or other coffee-flavored liqueur
1 pint vanilla ice cream
1 cup half-and-half
1/8 teaspoon almond extract
About 1-1/2 cups crushed ice

Combine all ingredients in container of electric blender. Blend until smooth. Yield: about 6 servings.

Brandied Peach Coffee

1/4 cup instant coffee powder, divided
5 cups cold water, divided
1/4 cup peach brandy, divided
4 scoops peach ice cream
Whipped cream
4 maraschino cherries

Place 2-1/2 teaspoons coffee powder in each of 4 (10-ounce) glasses. Set aside remaining coffee powder. Add 1/2 cup water to each glass, stirring until coffee dissolves. Stir in 3/4 cup water. Stir in 1 tablespoon brandy and add 1 scoop ice cream. Top each with whipped cream, 1/2 teaspoon coffee powder, and a cherry. Yield: 4 servings.

Vodka Slush

1 (6-ounce) can frozen orange juice concentrate, thawed and undiluted
2 (6-ounce) cans frozen lemonade concentrate, thawed and undiluted
2 (6-ounce) cans frozen limeade concentrate, thawed and undiluted
1 cup sugar
3-1/2 cups water
2 cups vodka
2 (28-ounce) bottles lemon-lime carbonated beverage, chilled

Combine first 6 ingredients, mixing well. Freeze 48 hours, stirring occasionally. For each serving, spoon 3/4 cup frozen mixture into a tall glass; fill with carbonated beverage. Serve at once. Yield: about 16 (8-ounce) servings.

Merry Brew

1/2 cup firmly packed brown sugar
1/4 teaspoon salt
2 sticks cinnamon
1 tablespoon whole cloves
1/2 teaspoon whole allspice
1 cup water
2 quarts apple juice
1 lemon, thinly sliced
1 orange, thinly sliced

Combine sugar, salt, spices, and water in a small saucepan; bring to a boil. Reduce heat, and simmer 10 minutes. Combine apple juice and fruit slices in a large suacepan; heat gently. Strain hot spice liquid into apple juice, and serve warm. Yield: 2 quarts.

Vincent van Gogh: Still Life with Potatoes in Yellow Dish, *1888, Kröller-Müller State Museum, The Netherlands*

The Essential Potato

It groweth naturally in Americus where it was first discovered . . .," wrote John Gerard of the potato in his *Herbal*. In the century between the discovery of "Americus" and botanist Gerard's observation in 1597, *solanum tuberosum*—the white potato—was to travel to Spain from its native Andes, to Virginia, and then to Ireland, where it was first planted in the late 1500's on Sir Walter Raleigh's estate. Acceptance of the potato in France was given great impetus by Antoine Parmentier who, as a prisoner-of-war in Prussia, had subsisted for five years on potatoes. Repatriated, Parmentier presented King Louis XVI with a basket of tubers, and the potato acceded to a top bin in the French kitchen. Hence the plaint in an English cookbook, ". . . why, while in France many dishes containing potatoes are called à la Parmentier, are there none in England named after Sir Walter Raleigh?" Raleigh's potatoes became the staple of Irish life—the "Irish Apple"—creating an overdependence which led to the tragic famine of 1846.

By the time of the "Great Hunger" in Ireland, the potato was basic to the diet of most of industrialized Europe. Into a dark corner of that society went young Vincent van Gogh in 1885, when he moved from his native Holland to live among the coal miners of southern Belgium. While sharing their meager lives he produced his first major painting—a brooding group portrait, *The Potato Eaters*. Later, van Gogh's palette and technique were changed radically by his exposure, in quick succession, to Paris and Impressionism. Fleeing the ferment of Paris, van Gogh escaped to the south of France where he burst forth with a great explosion of masterful painting. It ended two years later when van Gogh, tormented by episodic insanity, killed himself. In the spring of 1888, near the beginning of this extraordinary period, he rendered the dish of potatoes opposite, a painting literally light years away from his earlier portrayals of the same homely subject.　I.G.

Sweet potatoes—as a pie, candied and a casserole.
Photo by Kent Kirkley

Potatoes

"Needs salt," Queen Elizabeth is reputed to have said upon first tasting Raleigh's precious import from the New World. Since Good Queen Bess passed judgment, the homely spud and its kitchen companion, the sweet potato, have been improved upon in many ways. Here are some of them.

Potato Pancakes

4 large potatoes, peeled and chopped
1 large onion, chopped
2 eggs, beaten
1 tablespoon salad herbs
1/4 cup all-purpose flour
Salt and pepper to taste
Salad oil

Combine potatoes, onion, eggs, and herbs in container of an electric blender; blend at low speed until potatoes are grated. Combine potato mixture with flour, salt, and pepper.

Heat 1/4 inch salad oil in a large heavy skillet. Spoon 1/4 cup batter into oil to form a medium-size pancake. Fry until brown on one side; turn and fry until crisp. Repeat until all batter is used.

Serve with sour cream, catsup, or other favorite topping. Yield: about 20 pancakes.

Sesame Potato Sticks

6 to 8 medium baking potatoes, peeled
3/4 cup sesame seeds
1/2 cup melted butter or margarine
Salt
Paprika

Cut potatoes into strips 1 inch thick. Sprinkle sesame seeds in a thin layer on waxed paper. Dip potato sticks in butter; coat one side of sticks with sesame seeds. Place sticks, seed side up, on a well-greased baking sheet. Sprinkle with salt and paprika. Bake at 400° about 40 minutes or until done. Yield: about 8 servings.

Sweet Potato Pie

2 cups cooked, mashed sweet potatoes
1/2 cup butter or margarine, softened
2 eggs, separated
1 cup firmly packed brown sugar
1/4 teaspoon salt
1/2 teaspoon ground ginger
1/2 teaspoon ground cinnamon
1/2 teaspoon ground nutmeg
1/2 cup milk
1/4 cup sugar
1 unbaked 9-inch pastry shell
Additional spices (optional)
Whipped cream
Orange rind

Combine sweet potatoes, butter, egg yolks, brown sugar, salt, and spices; mix well. Add milk, blending until smooth.

Beat egg whites until foamy; gradually add 1/4 cup sugar, beating until stiff. Fold into sweet potato mixture. Pour filling into pastry shell; sprinkle with additional spices, if desired. Bake at 400° for 10 minutes. Reduce heat to 350°, and bake 30 additional minutes. When cool, garnish with whipped cream and orange rind. Yield: one 9-inch pie.

Potato Salad

1 medium onion
3 cups boiling water
1 teaspoon salt
6 medium potatoes, peeled and sliced
6 hard-cooked eggs, halved
1 cup sweet pickle cubes or relish
1 cup finely chopped celery
3/4 cup mayonnaise
2 tablespoons sweet pickle juice
3/4 teaspoon salt

Cut 2 slices from onion; place in boiling water. Finely chop remaining onion; set aside. Add 1 teaspoon salt and potatoes to water; cover and simmer 10 minutes or until done. Drain and cool.

Separate yolks and whites of eggs. Finely chop whites; combine with pickles, celery, and chopped onion.

Mash yolks; blend in mayonnaise, pickle juice, and 3/4 teaspoon salt, blending well. Combine yolk mixture with egg white mixture. Cube potatoes; blend into egg mixture. Cover and refrigerate several hours. Yield: 10 to 12 servings.

Holiday Scalloped Potatoes

2 tablespoons butter or margarine
3 tablespoons all-purpose flour
2 cups milk
3 cups diced cooked potatoes
2 tablespoons chopped parsley
2 tablespoons chopped pimiento
1-1/2 teaspoons salt
1/2 cup shredded Cheddar cheese
1/2 cup buttered breadcrumbs
1/4 teaspoon paprika

Melt butter in a heavy saucepan over low heat; gradually add flour. Cook until bubbly, stirring constantly. Gradually add milk; cook, stirring constantly, until thickened. Stir in potatoes, parsley, pimiento, and salt. Spoon into a greased 1-1/2-quart casserole.

Combine cheese, breadcrumbs, and paprika; sprinkle over potato mixture. Bake at 400° for 20 minutes. Yield: 4 to 6 servings.

Sweet Potato Rolls

3 cups whole wheat flour
3 cups all-purpose flour
2 packages dry yeast
1-1/2 cups warm water (105° to 115°)
1/3 cup firmly packed brown sugar
1-1/4 teaspoons salt
1/2 cup butter or margarine, softened
2 eggs
1 (9-ounce) can sweet potatoes, undrained

Combine flour, mixing well. Combine yeast and warm water in container of electric blender; process to dissolve yeast.

Add sugar, salt, butter, eggs, sweet potatoes, and 1 cup flour to yeast mixture; blend until smooth. Place remaining flour in large bowl; add yeast mixture, mixing to make a soft dough.

Turn dough out on a lightly floured board; knead about 5 minutes or until smooth and elastic. Place in a greased bowl, turning to grease top. Cover with plastic wrap, and refrigerate 6 hours or overnight.

About 1 hour before baking, divide dough in half. On a lightly floured surface, roll out each half into a 16-inch circle about 1/4 inch thick. Cut each circle into 16 wedges; roll up each wedge, beginning at widest edge.

Place wedges on greased baking sheets with the point on bottom. Cover and let rise in a warm place about 30 minutes or until light. Bake at 350° for 15 minutes. Yield: 32 rolls.

Cheese-Puffed Irish Potatoes

3 medium potatoes, peeled
2 tablespoons chopped onion
2/3 cup hot milk
2 eggs, separated
1 teaspoon salt
2 tablespoons butter or margarine
2 tablespoons chopped pimiento
1 cup shredded Cheddar cheese

Cut each potato into 3 pieces and place in a saucepan. Add onion, and cook, covered, in a small amount of boiling water 10 minutes or until done. Drain and mash; add milk, beaten egg yolks, salt, and butter, mixing well. Fold in pimiento, cheese, and stiffly beaten egg whites.

Pour into a greased 1-3/4-quart casserole, and bake at 350° for 25 to 30 minutes. Yield: 6 servings.

Sweet Potatoes with Orange Sauce

1/2 cup sugar
1/2 cup firmly packed brown sugar
2 tablespoons cornstarch
1/2 cup orange juice
1/4 cup melted butter or margarine
Salt to taste
4 or 5 medium-size sweet potatoes, sliced and cooked

Combine sugar and cornstarch; blend well. Stir in orange juice, butter, and salt. Simmer over low heat, stirring constantly, until slightly thickened.

Place potatoes in a lightly greased 2-quart casserole; add orange sauce. Bake at 350° for 30 minutes. Yield: 6 servings.

A pot in the form of a potato with deep eyes. Inca Period, National Museum, Lima

Candied Sweet Potatoes

4 medium or 3 large sweet potatoes
1/2 cup melted butter or margarine
1 cup sugar
1/4 cup water

Peel potatoes, and cut into 2-inch slices. Combine butter, sugar, and water in an electric skillet; add sweet potatoes. Cover and simmer at 250° for 1 hour or until done, turning frequently. Yield: 4 servings.

Sweet Potato Casserole

6 large sweet potatoes, cooked and peeled
1 cup butter, softened
Juice of 2 oranges
Grated rind of 2 oranges
4 eggs
1/2 to 1 cup sugar
Topping (recipe follows)

Beat sweet potatoes with electric mixer until fluffy. Add butter, orange juice and rind, eggs, and sugar; beat well. Spoon potato mixture into a 3-quart casserole. Cover with topping. Bake at 350° for 30 minutes. Yield: 8 to 10 servings.

Topping:
2 tablespoons butter
1 cup firmly packed brown sugar
2 tablespoons all-purpose flour
1 cup chopped pecans

Combine butter, sugar, and flour in a saucepan; cook over low heat until sugar melts, stirring constantly. Add pecans. Yield: about 1 cup.

Yummy Yams

4 pounds sweet potatoes, cooked and mashed
1/2 cup melted butter or margarine
1/4 cup bourbon
1/3 cup orange juice
1/3 cup firmly packed brown sugar
3/4 teaspoon salt
1/2 teaspoon apple pie spice
1/2 to 3/4 cup pecan halves

Combine all ingredients except pecans in a large mixing bowl, mixing well. Pour into a greased 2-1/2-quart casserole; arrange nuts around edge of dish. Bake at 350° for 45 minutes. Yield: 8 to 10 servings.

Herb Fried Potatoes

3 tablespoons butter or margarine
3 medium potatoes, pared and cut in 1/8-inch strips
1/2 teaspoon ground oregano
2 tablespoons chopped parsley
1/2 teaspoon instant minced onion
1/2 teaspoon salt
Pepper to taste

Melt butter in a 10-inch skillet; add potatoes. Cover and cook over medium heat 10 minutes. Turn potatoes carefully; cook, uncovered, 10 minutes more, turning occasionally to brown all sides. Sprinkle with remaining ingredients during last 5 minutes of cooking. Yield: 4 servings.

Party Stuffed Potatoes

6 baking potatoes
1/2 cup butter or margarine, softened
1 (8-ounce) carton commercial sour cream
1 (0.56-ounce) package bacon-onion dip mix
1 cup shredded Cheddar cheese
Salt and pepper to taste
Paprika

Scrub potatoes thoroughly. Bake at 425° for 40 to 60 minutes; allow to cool to touch. Slice skin away from most of one side of each potato. Carefully scoop out pulp, leaving shells intact.

Combine potato pulp, butter, sour cream, dip mix, cheese, salt, and pepper; whip until smooth.

Stuff shells with potato mixture; sprinkle with paprika. Bake at 350° for 25 minutes. Yield: 6 servings.

Old-Fashioned Potato Pie

1 unbaked 9-inch pastry shell
3 eggs, beaten
1 cup sugar
3/4 cup half-and-half
1 cup riced cooked potatoes
1 tablespoon vanilla extract
Ground nutmeg to taste (optional)

Bake pastry shell at 450° for 10 minutes; set aside.

Combine eggs, sugar, and half-and-half; beat well. Stir in potatoes and vanilla. Pour mixture into pastry shell; sprinkle with nutmeg, if desired. Bake at 350° for 30 minutes or until set. Yield: one 9-inch pie.

Lilly Martin Spencer:
Kiss Me and You'll
Kiss the 'Lasses,
1856,
Brooklyn Museum

Jams and Jellies, Pickles and Preserves

The meticulously stacked jars of preserves at right are the very symbol of old-fashioned thrift. Not many years ago, endless rows of sealed jars gleaming on the cellar shelves were the surest sign of a well-run home. Most of us have memories of torrid summer days when a bushel of some fruit or vegetable would arrive at the back door, and Mother's or Grandmother's kitchen would immediately be turned into a small factory. Children were especially useful on such occasions, since their hands were small enough to wash inside the jars. Though most modern households can survive nicely without putting up preserves, there are plenty of reasons other than economic for doing so: it is an excellent way of dealing with garden surplus; homemade relishes and preserves make fine—and appreciated—gifts; and it is fun. The pleasures of jelly-making is the subject of the painting opposite, rather coyly entitled *Kiss Me and You'll Kiss the 'Lasses,* by the American Victorian artist Lilly Martin Spencer. With all the good things on her table, this young woman will never find herself in the position of another Victorian lass, Lewis Carroll's Alice, who had a famous discussion with the White Queen on the subject:

"The rule is, jam tomorrow, and jam yesterday—but never jam today."

"It must come sometimes to jam today," Alice objected.

"No, it can't," said the Queen. "It's jam every other day: today isn't any other day, you know."

On this side of the looking glass, it often comes to jam today. Homemade jam, at that.

Pickles and relishes photographed by Taylor Lewis

73

Preserving

Pickled watermelon rind in December, fig preserves in February, peach-pecan jam in the teeth of a blue-norther—that's how to turn time on its heel. In the depth of winter, to taste last summer's conserve on warm toast is reassurance enough that spring will come again.

Strawberry-Fig Jam

4 cups figs
1-1/2 cups sugar
1 (3-ounce) package strawberry-flavored gelatin

Peel and mash figs; combine with sugar in a heavy saucepan. Cook over medium heat 2 minutes, stirring constantly. Gradually add gelatin, stirring constantly; cook and stir over low heat 15 minutes.

Spoon jam into hot, sterilized jars; seal and process 10 to 15 minutes in boiling-water bath. Yield: about 3 pints.

Note: Lemon-flavored gelatin may be substituted for strawberry.

Squash Pickles

8 cups sliced squash
2 cups sliced onion
1 tablespoon salt (not iodized)
1 cup diced green pepper
2 cups cider vinegar
3-1/2 cups sugar
1 teaspoon celery seeds
1 teaspoon mustard seeds

Combine squash and onion; sprinkle with salt, and let stand 1 hour. Combine green pepper, vinegar, sugar, celery seeds, and mustard seeds; bring to a boil.

Pack squash and onion into hot, sterilized jars; cover with vinegar mixture, and seal. Process in boiling-water bath 5 minutes. Yield: about 4 pints.

Muscadine grapes

Muscadine Jam

2 quarts muscadines
6 cups sugar

Remove stems and skins from muscadines. Cook pulp over low heat until soft; press through a sieve or food mill to remove seeds. Combine pulp and sugar in a large saucepan; cook over medium heat, stirring often until mixture boils. Boil about 10 minutes or almost to jellying point on candy thermometer; stir mixture frequently.

Remove from heat, and skim off foam with a metal spoon. Ladle quickly into sterilized jelly glasses, leaving 1/4-inch headspace. Seal at once with metal lids. Process in a boiling-water bath for 15 minutes. Yield: about 3 pints.

Note: Muscadine skins may be added to jam. Chop skins in a food processor or food chopper. Combine skins and about 1/2 cup water in a saucepan; simmer 15 to 20 minutes. Add to pulp and sugar and proceed as described.

Piccalilli

8 quarts green tomatoes, finely chopped
1 head cabbage, finely chopped
8 large onions, finely chopped
3 green peppers, finely chopped
1 cup pickling salt
2 quarts cider vinegar
1 (1-pound) package brown sugar
1 tablespoon mustard seeds
1 tablespoon ground cinnamon
2 tablespoons black pepper
1/4 teaspoon red pepper
1 tablespoon ground allspice
2 tablespoons ground ginger

Combine vegetables and salt; cover with water, and soak overnight. Drain and rinse vegetables.

Combine remaining ingredients, and bring to a boil; add drained vegetables, and return to a boil. Simmer 30 minutes or until vegetables are tender.

Pack hot mixture into sterilized jars; seal. Process in boiling-water bath 5 minutes. Yield: 16 pints.

Country Garden Relish

6 cups chopped green tomatoes
6 cups chopped red tomatoes
6 cups chopped cabbage
3 large onions, chopped
1/2 cup prepared horseradish
3 sweet peppers, chopped
1/2 cup salt
6 cups vinegar
5 cups sugar
1/2 teaspoon ground cinnamon
1/2 teaspoon ground cloves
1/2 cup mustard seeds

Combine tomatoes, cabbage, onion, horseradish, sweet pepper, and salt; refrigerate overnight. Drain; add remaining ingredients, and simmer 1 hour.

Pour hot relish into hot, sterilized jars, leaving 1/8-inch headspace. Seal and process 5 minutes in boiling-water bath. Yield: 3 quarts.

Peach-Pecan Jam

6 cups sliced fresh peaches
6 cups sugar
2/3 cup chopped pecans or walnuts

Combine peaches and sugar in a heavy saucepan; stir well. Bring to a boil. Reduce heat; simmer until thick (about 30 minutes), stirring occasionally. Remove from heat; stir in pecans. Spoon into sterilized jelly jars. Seal at once with 1/8-inch layer of hot paraffin; cover with lids. Yield: 6 half pints.

Note: Jam may be served over ice cream. Chill 8 hours before using as a topping.

Pepper Jelly

3/4 cup ground green pepper
1/4 cup ground hot pepper
6 cups sugar
1-1/2 cups white vinegar
1 (6-ounce) bottle liquid fruit pectin

Combine pepper, sugar, and vinegar in a large saucepan. Place over high heat, and stir until mixture comes to a hard boil. Boil hard 1 minute, stirring constantly.

Remove from heat; stir in pectin. Let sit 5 minutes. Skim off foam with a metal spoon, and pour quickly into sterilized jelly glasses. Seal at once with 1/8-inch layer of hot paraffin or metal lids. Yield: 6 half pints.

Watermelon Rind Pickles

1 watermelon
1 gallon water
1 cup pickling lime
1 quart vinegar
8 cups sugar
1 teaspoon pickling spices

Select a melon that has a thick rind. Remove outer green skin and pink flesh; use only the greenish-white parts of the rind. Cut rind into 1-inch cubes.

Combine water and lime; add cubed rind, and soak overnight in refrigerator.

Drain and rinse cubes in cold water several times. Then cover with cold water, and boil 30 minutes. Drain.

Combine vinegar, sugar, and pickling spices; cover cubes with this mixture. Boil slowly until cubes look clear (about 1 hour or longer), being sure cubes are covered with syrup throughout cooking. Add water if syrup cooks down.

Pack pickles in hot, sterilized jars; cover with syrup, and seal. Process in boiling-water bath 5 minutes. Yield: about 7 pints.

Fig Preserves

7 cups sugar
1/4 cup lemon juice
1-1/2 quarts hot water
2 quarts firm, ripe figs, peeled
2 lemons, thinly sliced

Combine sugar, lemon juice, and hot water in a large saucepan; cook over medium heat until sugar dissolves. Add figs and cook over high heat 10 minutes, stirring occasionally. Add lemons and continue cooking rapidly 10 to 15 minutes or until figs are clear. (If syrup becomes too thick before figs become clear, add boiling water, 1/4 cup at a time.)

Cover; let stand 12 to 24 hours in a cool place. Pack into sterilized jars, leaving 1/4-inch headspace; seal jars with metal lids. Process jars in a boiling-water bath for 30 minutes. Yield: about 10 half pints.

Note: Figs may be preserved without peeling, although the product will not be as high in quality. If unpeeled, figs should be covered with water, boiled for 15 to 20 minutes, and drained before adding to syrup.

Pepper-Onion Relish

2 quarts chopped red peppers (about 16 medium)
2 quarts chopped green peppers (about 16 medium)
1-1/2 cups chopped onion
2 teaspoons mixed pickling spices
1 hot pepper
1-1/2 cups vinegar
3/4 cup sugar
2 teaspoons salt (not iodized)

Combine vegetables, and cover with boiling water; let stand 5 minutes. Drain. Cover again with boiling water, and let stand 10 minutes; drain.

Tie spices and hot pepper in a cheesecloth bag. Combine vinegar, sugar, and salt; add spice bag, and simmer 15 minutes. Add vegetables, and simmer 10 minutes; remove spice bag.

Bring relish to boiling point. Pour boiling-hot relish into hot, sterilized jars, leaving 1/8-inch headspace. Adjust lids. Process 5 minutes in boiling-water bath. Yield: about 6 half pints.

Blackberry Jelly

About 3 quarts ripe blackberries
7-1/2 cups sugar
1 (6-ounce) bottle liquid fruit pectin

Sort and wash berries; remove stems and caps. Crush berries to extract 4 cups juice. Combine juice and sugar in a large saucepan, and mix well. Place over high heat; cook, stirring constantly, until mixture comes to a rapid boil. Boil hard 1 minute, stirring constantly. Add pectin, and bring to a full rolling boil; boil 1 minute, stirring constantly.

Remove from heat, and skim off foam with a metal spoon. Pour jelly quickly into sterilized glasses, leaving 1/2-inch headspace. Cover at once with metal lids or 1/2-inch layer of hot paraffin. Yield: about 8 to 9 half pints.

Strawberry Freezer Jam

About 1 quart fully ripe strawberries
3 cups sugar
1 cup light corn syrup
1 (1-3/4-ounce) package powdered fruit pectin
3/4 cup water

Wash and stem strawberries. Thoroughly crush berries, one layer at a time, to let juice flow freely. Measure 2 cups crushed berries into a bowl. Add sugar and corn syrup; stir thoroughly.

Combine fruit pectin and water in a small saucepan; bring to boil over medium heat, stirring constantly until fruit pectin is dissolved. Boil 1 minute. Pour into strawberry mixture; stir 3 minutes. Quickly ladle into sterilized jars or freezer containers. Cover at once with tight lids.

Let stand at room temperature until set (this may take up to 24 hours); then store in freezer. When jam is to be used, remove from freezer and store in refrigerator. Yield: 6 half pints.

Zucchini Pickles

2 pounds fresh, firm zucchini
2 small onions
1/4 cup pickling salt
2 cups sugar
1 teaspoon celery salt
1 teaspoon turmeric
2 teaspoons mustard seeds
3 cups cider vinegar

Wash zucchini, and cut into thin slices. Cut onions into quarters; then slice very thin. Combine zucchini and onion; cover with 1 inch of water, add pickling salt. Let stand 2 hours; drain.

Combine remaining ingredients and bring to a boil. Pour over zucchini and onion, and let stand 2 hours. Bring mixture to a boil, and simmer 5 minutes. Pack while hot into sterilized jars, leaving 1/8-inch headspace. Process in boiling-water bath 15 minutes. Yield: about 3 pints.

Blackberries by Raphaelle Peale. Fine Arts Museums of San Francisco, de Young Memorial

Edouard Manet: Oysters, *1862, National Gallery of Art, Washington, D.C.*

Shore Things

The linguistic possibilities of shellfish have long been apparent. Oysters have a lore all their own: they must be eaten only in months that contain "R" (September through April); pearls are not invariably to be found in them; and if the world is one's oyster it's likely to result in being happy as a clam. Oysters (the ones at right were photographed in a New Orleans courtyard) are probably the king of shellfish, or perhaps the queen — for this curious bivalve changes sex willy-nilly. One of the best descriptions of oyster habits is in M. F. K. Fisher's *The Art of Eating* (Vintage Books, 1976). "An oyster," she writes, "leads a dreadful but exciting life." It hatches out as a microscopic dot of protoplasm in the ocean, and only after many days of free floating does it take hold of a rock and build itself a shell. It may then become the parent of millions of little oysters — sometimes as the father, sometimes as the mother. Man is his or her worst enemy. "Its chilly, delicate gray body slips into a stew-pan or under a broiler or alive down a red throat, and it is done. Its life has been thoughtless but no less full of danger, and now that it is over we are perhaps the better for it."

The live oysters in their shells, opposite, painted by Edouard Manet, look almost edible — they need only a squeeze of lemon. Manet, who is often linked with the Impressionist painters of his time, stayed closer to the tradition of classic French realism than they did. Like many fine still-lifes, *Oysters* is a bravura exercise — a compliment as much to the skill of the artist and the magical power of oil paint as to the mollusk portrayed.

Oysters en Brochette, Bienville, Rockefeller, Commander and in a loaf — photographed in a New Orleans courtyard by Kent Kirkley

Benvenuto Cellini: **Gold Saltcellar**, *1540, Kunsthistorisches Museum, Vienna*

Herbs, Spices, Seasonings

A hundred times more divine a thing than I had ever dreamed of." So Francis I, King of France, exclaimed when presented with a model of this golden saltcellar in 1543—at least, according to the goldsmith, Benvenuto Cellini. Cellini was not only one of the master craftsmen of the Italian Renaissance but was also a master at self-promotion. The god and goddess on the lid of the boat-shaped container, thirteen inches long, represent the sea (salt) and the land (pepper). And if the effect is faintly erotic, as well as symbolic, the King surely did not object. The triple arch beside the goddess held the pepper; the salt was kept under the lid. One might imagine that the creator and the users of such a precious object were the most refined of courtiers. Yet, when he arrived in France to make the saltcellar, Cellini had just done a stretch in an Italian jail and was in exile from his native Florence for duelling. As to the table manners of a typical Renaissance prince, they were dependably inelegant. Knives and forks were seldom used, bones and leavings were thrown to the floor. Etiquette books of the day cautioned noble banqueters not to wipe their greasy fingers on the bread, or blow their noses in their napkins, or scratch their nether parts. Moreover, salt and pepper—in addition to spices and herbs (most of the seasonings at right were well known in the Renaissance) —were used for disguising inferior foods, rather than enhancing good ones. None of this, of course, detracts one whit from Cellini's saltcellar, one of the great masterpieces of Western craft.

Ham and seasonings photographed by Phillip Kretchmar

دو پیکان نهاده پس و پیش سر
بجوان مردرون شک گشته تیر پش

بجم کنان مهره دو مهره داست
پسند آتش مو و جای سپید

هیسور اسوی حبت و گیر نبا
بگوش علی آمو اندر کنب

بخارید گوش آمو اندر زبا
سروکوش پایش مسکان حبت

بیمرا مدرون آمد جاجی کمال
برای آواز آزاده رادل بسوخت

هسیمون ابر بر ماه جهن برآ
برد دست و جمکش بحون درشا

Call of the Wild

The first human beings were hunters, and people continued to hunt even after they started farming. Hunting cuts across all class lines. Aristocrats have traditionally hunted for sport, and others from need. Until very recent times in many nations, wild meat was the only kind to be had. In frontier America, for example—particularly in the South—game in some form was likely to be part of everybody's weekly fare.

The hunter in the Persian miniature opposite is in graceful pursuit of a venison stew, though surely not out of necessity. He is Shah Bahram Gur, ruler of Persia in the fifth century A.D. His mistress, Azada, riding sedately behind the Shah and strumming a lute, has presumably challenged her lover to pin the hoof of a deer to its ear with one shot of the bow. And since such tales must end happily, he is about to succeed. Meanwhile, game of all kinds bounds through the dainty landscape—rabbits, deer, wild goats—and a bear growls in his cave. The painting was made in 1614, long after Bahram and Azada had faded into the national mythology, as an illumination for a Book of Kings in honor of a later potentate, Shah Abbas the Great.

According to Brillat-Savarin, the nineteenth-century French authority on gastronomy, game is a food at once "healthy, warming, savorous, and stimulating to the taste, and is easily assimilated by anyone with a youthful digestive apparatus." But, as he also remarks, the skill of the cook is critical. The venison, quail, and wild duck at right, as well as other wild meats, need to be handled in special ways. But the rewards are worth the effort.

Venison with Sour Cream, Quail in Red Wine, and Stuffed Wild Duck. Photo by Kent Kirkley

Wild Game

Quail, duck, deer, and dove taken in rice field, swamp, plain, and woodland—a wild bounty from a richly varied landscape.

Venison Fillets

Cut the venison tenderloin into fillets 1-1/2 inches thick. Wrap a thick slice of bacon around each fillet. Place fillets on a grill. Cook over hot coals about 10 minutes on each side or to medium doneness, basting frequently with butter or margarine. Do not overcook. Season with salt and pepper to taste.

Venison Bourguignon

5 medium onions, sliced
1 (8-ounce) package fresh mushrooms, sliced
2 tablespoons melted shortening or vegetable oil
2 pounds venison steak, cut into 1-inch cubes
1 teaspoon salt
1/4 teaspoon marjoram
1/4 teaspoon thyme
1/8 teaspoon pepper
1-1/2 tablespoons all-purpose flour
3/4 cup beef bouillon
1-1/2 cups Burgundy
Hot cooked rice or toasted French bread

Sauté onion and mushrooms in shortening until tender. Drain on absorbent towels, reserving drippings; set vegetables aside.

Brown meat in pan drippings; add additional shortening, if needed. Remove pan from heat; sprinkle seasonings over meat.

Combine flour and bouillon, stirring well; pour over meat and boil 1 minute, stirring constantly. Stir in Burgundy; cover and simmer 1-1/2 to 2 hours or until meat is tender. Stir in mushrooms and onions; simmer, uncovered, 15 minutes.

Transfer to a chafing dish set over low heat. Serve over rice or in bowls with toasted French bread. Yield: 6 to 8 servings.

Venison with Sour Cream

2 pounds venison, cut in 2-inch cubes
1 clove garlic, minced
1/4 cup shortening, melted
1 cup diced celery
1/2 cup chopped onion
1 cup diced carrots
2 cups water
1 teaspoon salt
Dash of pepper
1 bay leaf
4 tablespoons melted butter or margarine
4 tablespoons all-purpose flour
1 cup commercial sour cream
Parsley

Place venison, garlic, and shortening in a skillet; brown meat on all sides over medium heat. Remove meat to a shallow 2-1/2-quart baking dish.

Add celery, onion, and carrots to drippings in skillet; sauté 2 minutes. Stir in water, salt, pepper, and bay leaf; pour over venison. Bake at 350° for 30 minutes; remove from oven. Drain, reserving broth.

Combine butter and flour in a skillet; cook over low heat, stirring until smooth. Add reserved broth; cook until thickened, stirring constantly. Stir in sour cream. Pour sauce over venison and vegetables. Garnish with parsley. Yield: 6 to 8 servings.

Stuffed Wild Duck

1 young, plump wild duck, cleaned
Salt
1/3 cup chopped celery
1/2 cup unpeeled chopped apple
1 small onion, chopped
3 tablespoons melted shortening or bacon
  drippings
2/3 cup water
1/3 cup orange juice
Parsley, grapes, apple wedges

Rub cavity of duck with 1 teaspoon salt. Combine celery, apple, and onion; stuff into cavity of duck. Close cavity with skewers.

Brown duck in shortening in a heavy Dutch oven; add water, orange juice, and 1/4 teaspoon salt. Cover tightly; cook over low heat 45 minutes to 1 hour or until tender. (Cooking time depends on age of duck.) Baste 2 or 3 times during cooking. Garnish with parsley, grapes, and apple. Yield: 3 servings.

Venison Curry

1 leg venison
3 (1/2-inch-thick) ham slices
2 large onions, chopped
1 cup raisins or currants
6 tablespoons curry powder
2 cups beef broth
Cooked rice
3/4 cup diced celery
4 lemons or limes, halved
Paprika
Chopped parsley

Place venison, fat side up, on rack in roasting pan. Do not season or add water. Roast, uncovered, at 325° for 20 to 25 minutes per pound. Allow to cool; cut into cubes. Fry ham, and reserve drippings; cut ham into cubes.

Sauté onion in reserved ham drippings until transparent. Add venison and ham; sauté an additional 5 minutes. Add raisins, curry powder, and beef broth; simmer, uncovered, 30 minutes. Add additional curry powder or broth if needed.

Spoon rice onto a large serving platter, shaping into a ring; add curry, and sprinkle with celery. Dip lemon halves in paprika, and sprinkle with parsley; use to garnish curry.

Serve curry with several of the following condiments: flaked coconut, almonds, pineapple chunks, chutney, bacon chips, banana slices, and chopped hard-cooked egg. Yield: about 10 to 12 servings.

Standing on a papyrus boat which floats on water teeming with fish, a hunter captures wild fowl. Scene from the tomb of Nebamen. XVIII Dynasty, c. 1400 B.C. Permission of the Trustees of the British Museum

Roast Wild Duck with Chestnut Dressing

8 chestnuts, mashed
1/4 cup melted butter
1/2 cup breadcrumbs
1/2 cup milk
1/4 cup diced celery
1 or 2 shallots, diced
Pinch of sage
Pinch of rosemary
1/4 cup white seedless raisins
Salt and pepper to taste
1 (2- to 3-pound) mallard duck
Clove garlic
Ground ginger
3 bacon slices

Combine chestnuts, butter, breadcrumbs, milk, celery, shallots, sage, rosemary, raisins, salt, and pepper; mix dressing well.

Season cavity of duck with salt and pepper; rub outside with garlic, and sprinkle with ginger. Stuff cavity with dressing mixture; place bacon over breast.

Preheat oven to 450°; place duck in oven, and reduce oven temperature to 350°. Roast 30 minutes, basting frequently. Remove bacon. Roast duck 30 minutes longer, basting frequently.

Remove dressing from cavity before serving. Serve dressing separately. Yield: 4 servings.

Venison Roast

1 (5-pound) venison roast
Salt and pepper
4 teaspoons beef stock base
2 cups water
1 (16-ounce) carton commercial sour cream

Rub roast with salt and pepper. Brown roast in a skillet. Place in a roasting pan; roast, uncovered, at 350° about 2 hours or until medium doneness, basting frequently. (Roasting time will depend on age of venison; older venison will need to cook longer.)

Remove roast from oven. Combine stock base and water, stirring to dissolve. Blend stock into sour cream, and pour over roast. Bake at 300° for 20 to 30 minutes, basting frequently. Yield: about 8 servings.

Country-Style Quail

6 quail, cleaned and split down back
1/4 cup all-purpose flour
1 teaspoon salt
1/2 teaspoon pepper
Vegetable oil
3 tablespoons all-purpose flour
1 cup water
1/2 teaspoon salt
Hot cooked rice

Spread quail open; pat dry with paper towels. Combine 1/4 cup flour, 1 teaspoon salt, and pepper; dredge quail in flour mixture. Heat 1/4 inch of oil in a skillet; place quail in skillet, and brown on both sides, turning once. Remove from skillet.

Combine 3 tablespoons flour, 1 cup water, and 1/2 teaspoon salt; stir until smooth. Blend into drippings in skillet. Place quail in gravy, and add enough water to half cover birds. Cover; reduce heat to low, and simmer 30 minutes or until tender. Serve birds, breast side up, over hot cooked rice. Yield: 6 servings.

Quail in Red Wine

6 quail, cleaned
Brandy
All-purpose flour
6 tablespoons butter or margarine
2 cups sliced mushrooms
1/4 cup melted butter or margarine
1 cup consommé
1 cup dry red wine
1 stalk celery, quartered
Salt and pepper
Juice of 2 oranges, strained
Cooked wild rice

Rub quail with a cloth soaked in brandy, and dust with flour. Melt 6 tablespoons butter in a heavy skillet; add quail, and sauté 10 minutes.

Sauté mushrooms in 1/4 cup butter; pour over quail. Add consommé, wine, celery, salt, and pepper. Cover and simmer 20 to 30 minutes or until quail is tender. Discard celery, if desired; stir in orange juice. Heat thoroughly. Serve with wild rice. Yield: 6 servings.

Saucy Dove

About 1 cup all-purpose flour
1-1/4 teaspoons salt
1/4 teaspoon pepper
1/2 teaspoon poultry seasoning
12 to 15 medium doves, cleaned
1/2 cup melted butter or margarine
1 (8-ounce) can tomato sauce
1 (4-ounce) can mushroom stems and pieces, drained
1 large onion, diced
About 1/3 cup milk

Combine flour, salt, pepper, and poultry seasoning in a bag; add doves and shake to coat birds well. Brown doves in butter in a large skillet. Add tomato sauce, mushrooms, and onion. Cover and cook over low heat until tender, about 20 minutes. Remove doves, and keep warm.

Add milk to pan drippings, scraping sides and bottom of skillet. Heat, stirring constantly, to make a sauce; spoon over doves. Yield: about 6 servings.

Note: Quail may be used instead of dove.

Doves the Easy Way

12 medium doves, cleaned
1/2 teaspoon seasoned salt
1/2 teaspoon salt
1/4 teaspoon freshly ground black pepper
1 cup water, divided
1/2 cup melted butter or margarine
2 tablespoons lemon juice
1 tablespoon all-purpose flour
Cooked wild rice

Do not wash doves unless necessary, and then very quickly. Wipe with a clean, damp cloth or paper towels. Place doves in a large iron skillet. Combine salt and pepper; sprinkle over doves.

Pour 1/2 cup water into skillet; cover tightly, and steam over medium heat 20 minutes. Remove lid, and continue cooking until all water is gone.

Add butter and lemon juice to skillet. Continue cooking until doves are brown on all sides, turning occasionally; remove doves from skillet, and place in a casserole.

Add flour to drippings in skillet, stirring until smooth; cook over low heat until lightly browned. Add remaining 1/2 cup water; cook until thickened, stirring constantly. Pour gravy over doves; serve with wild rice. Yield: 6 servings.

Anonymous:
Pasta Merchant,
undated,
Museo Storica
Degli Spaghetti,
Pontedassio,
Italy

A Passion for Pasta

There are as many shapes of pasta as the human imagination can devise. Long and thin, short and fat, solid string and hollow pipe, stars, shells, slabs, curlicues, dots, and stripes. The possibilities are limitless, and nearly every wheat-growing nation eats pasta of some kind. Along with dried meat, it was undoubtedly one of the earliest convenience foods, for it compactly preserves the nourishing but perishable commodity of wheat. All that is needed to reconvert it into something edible is a pot of boiling water. Just who invented pasta, and when, has been a subject of international dispute. The Chinese claim that they did, and insist that Marco Polo brought noodles back from Hangchow to Venice in the late thirteenth century. The Italians say that, on the contrary, they have been making and eating pasta since the beginning of time. In any case, the pasta merchant opposite, portrayed by an anonymous Neapolitan artist, clearly could not care less. As the prices posted on his bins of pasta show, he is part of a retail operation, and in the back of his shop the pasta is presumably being mass-produced. (One technique probably employed was kneading the dough by foot.) He appears to be holding a bunch of wet spaghetti on a stick, but in fact it is only a fly swatter made of string.

Whatever form it may take, pasta was long ago assimilated into American cooking, a naturalized citizen whose name may be Italian but whose home ground now definitely includes the United States.

Varieties of pasta photographed by Charles Beck

89

Pasta

Pasta comes in an infinity of forms—spaghetti, linguini, manicotti, fettucini—some difficult to pronounce, all wonderful to eat.

Four-Cheese Spaghetti

1 (12-ounce) package spaghetti
1-1/2 teaspoons all-purpose flour
3 tablespoons melted butter or margarine
1 cup half-and-half
3/4 cup shredded provolone cheese
3/4 cup shredded Swiss cheese
3/4 cup shredded Edam or Gouda cheese
1/4 cup grated Parmesan cheese
1/2 teaspoon salt
1/8 teaspoon pepper
1 teaspoon dried basil or 1 tablespoon chopped fresh basil

Cook spaghetti according to package directions; drain well, and keep warm.

Stir flour into butter; cook over low heat, stirring constantly, until bubbly. Gradually add half-and-half; cook over low heat, stirring constantly, until smooth and thickened.

Add cheese, salt, and pepper to white sauce; stir constantly until cheese melts. Pour cheese sauce over spaghetti, tossing to evenly coat spaghetti. Sprinkle with basil; serve immediately. Yield: 6 to 8 servings.

Cheesy Green Noodles

2 cups spinach noodles
3 tablespoons melted butter or margarine
1/8 teaspoon garlic powder
3 tablespoons grated Parmesan cheese
3 tablespoons shredded Swiss cheese
Freshly ground black pepper

Cook noodles according to package directions; drain. Combine butter and garlic powder; add noodles, mixing well. Sprinkle with cheese and pepper. Serve immediately. Yield: 2 servings.

Noodles Romanoff

1-1/2 tablespoons salt
5 quarts boiling water
1 (12-ounce) package 1/2-inch-wide noodles
1 (24-ounce) carton creamed cottage cheese
2 (8-ounce) cartons commercial sour cream
6 tablespoons melted butter or margarine, divided
1-1/2 cups chopped green onions
1 clove garlic, crushed
1/4 teaspoon pepper
1/2 cup fine breadcrumbs

Add salt to rapidly boiling water; add noodles gradually so that water continues to boil. Cook, uncovered, for 7 minutes; stir occasionally. Drain; set aside.

Combine cottage cheese, sour cream, 4 tablespoons butter, onion, garlic, and pepper. Add noodles and toss lightly with a fork. Spoon into a lightly greased 4-quart casserole.

Combine breadcrumbs and remaining 2 tablespoons butter, stirring well; sprinkle over noodles. Bake at 350° for 25 to 30 minutes. Yield: 10 to 12 servings.

Pizza Spaghetti

1 cup shredded Swiss cheese
1 pound mozzarella cheese, shredded
1-1/2 pounds ground beef
Salt to taste
1 medium onion, chopped
2 (6-ounce) cans tomato paste
2/3 cup water
1 (4-ounce) can mushroom stems and pieces, undrained
1/2 teaspoon oregano
1 (6-ounce) package vermicelli
1/4 cup melted margarine

Combine cheeses and set aside.

Combine ground beef and salt; sauté until meat is done, stirring to crumble well. Add onion, and sauté until tender; drain well. Stir in tomato paste, water, mushrooms, and oregano.

Cook vermicelli according to package directions; drain. Combine vermicelli and margarine, tossing well; add to meat sauce.

Reserve 1 cup cheese mixture; combine remaining cheese with meat mixture. Spoon into a greased 2-1/2-quart casserole; sprinkle with reserved cheese. Bake at 350° for 20 to 30 minutes or until bubbly. Yield: 6 servings.

Linguini with Clam Sauce

1 (16-ounce) package linguini
3 cloves garlic
1 cup melted butter or margarine
2 (7-1/2-ounce) cans minced clams, undrained
1/2 cup chopped parsley
1/4 teaspoon crushed basil
1/4 teaspoon thyme

Cook linguini according to package directions; drain.

Sauté garlic in butter over low heat until brown; discard garlic. Add clams, and heat thoroughly. Stir in parsley, basil, and thyme. Serve over linguini. Yield: about 6 servings.

Three-Cheese Manicotti

1-1/2 cups water
1 (8-ounce) can tomato sauce
1 (1-1/2-ounce) package spaghetti sauce mix
2 cups shredded mozzarella cheese, divided
1 cup ricotta or small-curd cottage cheese
1/2 cup grated Parmesan cheese
2 eggs, beaten
1/2 teaspoon salt
1/8 teaspoon pepper
8 manicotti shells

Combine water, tomato sauce, and spaghetti sauce mix in a small saucepan. Simmer, uncovered, 10 minutes.

Combine 1 cup mozzarella cheese, ricotta, Parmesan, eggs, salt, and pepper; stir gently, and set aside.

Cook manicotti shells according to package directions; drain. Stuff cheese mixture into manicotti shells, using about 1/4 cup for each shell.

Pour 1/2 cup sauce into a shallow 2-quart casserole; arrange manicotti shells in sauce, and pour remaining sauce over top. Sprinkle with remaining mozzarella cheese. Bake, uncovered, at 350° for 25 to 30 minutes or until bubbly. Yield: 4 servings.

Macaroni Croquettes

6 tablespoons melted butter or margarine
6 tablespoons all-purpose flour
2 cups half-and-half or milk
1 teaspoon salt
1/4 teaspoon white pepper
1 (8-ounce) package elbow macaroni, cooked and
  drained
3 cups shredded sharp Cheddar cheese
Cracker meal
Hot vegetable oil

Combine butter and flour; cook over low heat, stirring constantly, until smooth and bubbly. Gradually add half-and-half; cook, stirring constantly, until smooth and thickened. Stir in salt, pepper, macaroni, and cheese. Let cool.

Drop macaroni mixture by tablespoonfuls onto a cookie sheet; chill until easy to handle. Shape into croquettes, and roll each in cracker meal. Place in refrigerator overnight or until firm.

Brown croquettes in vegetable oil; drain well. Yield: about 30 croquettes.

Quick-and-Easy Lasagna

1 to 1-1/2 pounds ground beef
1 (15-1/2-ounce) can spaghetti sauce with
  mushrooms
2 (8-ounce) cans tomato sauce
1 (8-ounce) can tomato sauce with mushrooms
1 teaspoon oregano
1 tablespoon instant minced onion
1 clove garlic, minced
1 (8-ounce) can sliced mushrooms, drained
1 (8-ounce) package lasagna noodles
1 (16-ounce) carton ricotta or creamed cottage
  cheese
1/2 pound mozzarella cheese, thinly sliced
1/2 cup grated Parmesan cheese

Sauté ground beef until lightly browned; drain off drippings. Add spaghetti sauce, tomato sauces, oregano, onion, garlic, and mushrooms; bring to a boil. Lower heat; cover and simmer 15 minutes.

Cook noodles according to package directions; drain.

Spoon one-third of meat sauce into a shallow greased 2-1/2-quart casserole. Top with half the lasagna, half of ricotta, and half of mozzarella. Repeat layers, and top with remaining meat sauce; sprinkle with Parmesan. Bake at 350° for 40 minutes. Yield: 8 servings.

An early Italian illumination of two women gathering spinach leaves, New York Public Library

Layered Pasta Florentine

1 (10-ounce) package frozen chopped spinach
1 pound ground beef
1 medium onion, chopped
1 clove garlic, minced
1 tablespoon hot vegetable oil
1 (15-1/2-ounce) jar spaghetti sauce with
  mushrooms
1 (8-ounce) can tomato sauce
1 (6-ounce) can tomato paste
1/2 teaspoon salt
Dash of pepper
1 (8-ounce) package seashell macaroni
1 cup shredded sharp process American cheese
1/2 cup breadcrumbs
2 eggs, well beaten
1/2 cup vegetable oil

Cook spinach according to package directions. Drain, reserving liquid. Add enough water to spinach liquid to make 1 cup; set aside spinach and liquid.

Brown ground beef, onion, and garlic in 1 tablespoon oil; stir to crumble beef. Stir spinach liquid, spaghetti sauce, tomato sauce, tomato paste, salt, and pepper into meat mixture; simmer 10 minutes. Set aside.

Cook macaroni according to package directions; drain. Combine macaroni, spinach, cheese, breadcrumbs, eggs, and 1/2 cup oil; stir gently to mix well. Spread evenly in a lightly greased 13-1/2- x 8-3/4- x 1-3/4-inch baking dish; top with meat sauce. Bake at 350° for 30 minutes. Yield: 8 to 10 servings.

Chicken and Vermicelli Soup

1 (1- to 1-1/2-pound) chicken, cut in serving-size
  pieces
9 cups boiling water
1-1/2 teaspoons freshly ground black pepper
1 teaspoon salt
1/2 teaspoon crushed thyme
1 bay leaf
1 teaspoon chopped parsley
1 medium onion, chopped
1/3 pound fresh mushrooms, sliced
2 tablespoons white wine
1 teaspoon lemon juice
2 teaspoons butter or margarine
Salt and pepper to taste
1 (7-ounce) package vermicelli

Add chicken to boiling water; stir in next 6 ingredients, and cook until meat pulls away from bones. Remove chicken from broth; cool, and cut meat into bite-size pieces.

Combine mushrooms, wine, lemon juice, and butter; cook until mushrooms are tender. Season to taste with salt and pepper. Add mushroom mixture to broth along with meat and vermicelli; cook until vermicelli is tender. Yield: 8 to 10 servings.

Chicken Spaghetti

1 (3- to 4-pound) hen
1 (12-ounce) package thin spaghetti
1 green pepper, chopped
1 medium onion, chopped
1/2 cup chopped celery
1/2 cup pitted ripe olives, sliced
1/2 cup green olives, sliced
2 tablespoons melted margarine
1 tablespoon sherry
2 (10-1/2-ounce) cans cream of mushroom soup,
  undiluted
1 cup chicken broth
1/2 cup grated Parmesan cheese

Cook hen until tender; bone and cut into bite-size pieces. Cook spaghetti according to package directions; drain and set aside.

Sauté green pepper, onion, celery, and olives in margarine and set aside.

Mix sherry with soup. Stir in cooked spaghetti. Add enough chicken broth to make a smooth consistency. Add the sautéed ingredients and the cooked chicken. Put in a greased 2-1/2-quart casserole dish. Sprinkle Parmesan cheese on top. Bake at 350° for 20 minutes. Yield: 8 to 10 servings.

Kees van Dongen: **The Picnic at Louvard**, *1924, Private collection*

Dinner on the Ground

No one is quite sure where the word came from, but a picnic—strictly speaking—is an outdoor party to which all the participants bring something to eat. The culture of the South has an especially rich tradition of gatherings conforming to this definition: all-day-singings-and-dinners-on-the-ground, barbecues, reunions, cornhusking bees, and covered-dish socials of all kinds. Aside from its obvious virtues as a participatory sport, a picnic is also a fine way to retreat from the world (as at right) or, by contrast, a lavish and elegant way to entertain (as opposite). The sophisticated picnickers at this gathering, which took place in the summer of 1924, are at a hunting lodge near Paris owned by Kees van Dongen, who not only gave the party but painted the picture as well. Van Dongen, a Dutch artist, left his homeland as a young man, in 1897, and took up *la vie de bohème* in Montmartre. He played the role of starving artist to the hilt, but after a few years found himself famous, even rich: Kiki van Dongen, the court painter of the smart set. One of his specialties was dancing the Charleston; another was portraying chic Parisiennes. The decorative woman at center, wearing a sailor dress and a large hat, was his companion, Madame Jasmy. There is no record of what the guests had for lunch that day. Obviously there was plenty of champagne.

A perfect picnic photographed by Taylor Lewis

Picnics

A jaded gourmand once said, "A picnic is when you've forgotten something essential." The basic basket for two as well as the extended family outing can profitably include any of the following—but don't forget the ice!

Southern Fried Chicken

1/2 pound salt pork, cut into 1/4-inch slices
Vegetable oil
3/4 cup all-purpose flour
1/2 teaspoon salt
1/8 teaspoon pepper
1 tablespoon paprika
1 (2- to 3-pound) broiler-fryer chicken, cut up

Sauté salt pork until brown, and remove from skillet; add oil to drippings to a depth of 1 inch.

Combine flour, salt, pepper, and paprika; dredge chicken in flour mixture. Brown chicken on both sides in hot oil mixture. Cover; reduce heat to medium, and fry about 20 minutes or until tender. Drain on paper towels. Yield: 4 servings.

Super Rice Salad

1-1/2 cups water
1-1/2 cups instant rice
1/2 cup chopped celery
1/4 cup chopped dill pickle
1 tablespoon chopped onion
1 tablespoon chopped parsley
1/2 teaspoon dry mustard
1 cup mayonnaise
Salt and pepper to taste
Hard-cooked egg slices or stuffed olive slices

Bring water to a boil, and stir in rice. Cover; remove from heat, and let stand 5 minutes. Add celery, dill pickle, onion, parsley, mustard, and mayonnaise; chill at least 1 hour. Add salt and pepper to taste, and garnish with egg or olive slices. Yield: 6 servings.

Picnic Potato Salad

5 pounds potatoes, cooked and cubed
1 cup sliced green onions
1/2 cup commercial Italian dressing
1 cup mayonnaise or salad dressing
1/4 cup prepared mustard
3 teaspoons salt
2 cups sliced celery
4 hard-cooked eggs, chopped
1/2 cup sweet pickle relish
Parsley
Green pepper rings

Combine potatoes, onion, and Italian dressing; toss gently to coat. Cover and chill 1 hour. Combine mayonnaise, mustard, and salt; pour over potato mixture; toss gently to coat. Add celery, eggs, and relish; toss lightly. Chill several hours. Garnish with parsley and green pepper rings. Yield: 10 to 12 servings.

Florentine Franks

2 tomatoes, peeled, chopped, and drained
4 tablespoons shredded sharp American cheese
2 small cloves garlic, crushed
1/2 teaspoon crushed oregano leaves
Salt to taste
8 frankfurters
8 slices bacon
8 hotdog buns, split and toasted

Combine tomato, cheese, garlic, oregano, and salt; mix well. Split frankfurters lengthwise, cutting almost through; stuff with tomato mixture.

Wrap each frankfurter with a bacon strip, securing ends with toothpicks. Place franks over medium coals; grill 10 to 15 minutes or until bacon is crisp, turning occasionally. Serve in buns. Yield: 6 to 8 servings.

Cheese Deviled Eggs

6 hard-cooked eggs
3 tablespoons shredded sharp Cheddar cheese
1-1/2 tablespoons vinegar
1/2 teaspoon prepared mustard
1/2 teaspoon salt
1/2 teaspoon pepper
2 tablespoons butter or margarine, softened

Slice eggs in half lengthwise, and carefully remove yolks. Mash yolks; blend in remaining ingredients. Stuff egg whites with yolk mixture. Yield: 6 servings.

Stuffed Hamburgers

2 tablespoons butter or margarine
1-1/4 cups herb-seasoned stuffing
1 egg, beaten
1 (4-ounce) can chopped mushrooms, drained
1/3 cup beef broth
1/4 cup sliced green onion
1/4 cup chopped toasted almonds
1 teaspoon lemon juice
3 pounds ground beef
1 teaspoon salt

Melt butter in a saucepan over low heat; remove from heat. Add stuffing, egg, mushrooms, beef broth, green onion, almonds, and lemon juice; mix well, and set aside. Combine ground beef and salt; shape into 16 patties.

Top 8 patties with stuffing mixture, using 1/4 cup per patty. Cover with remaining patties; pinch edges together to seal. Place patties in greased grill basket. Grill over medium coals for 10 to 12 minutes on each side. Yield: 6 to 8 servings.

Crispy Slaw

1 medium head cabbage, shredded
1 small onion, chopped
1 green pepper, chopped
1 cup sugar
1 cup vinegar
1 teaspoon salt
1 teaspoon mustard seeds
1 teaspoon celery seeds
1/4 teaspoon ground turmeric

Combine cabbage, onion, and green pepper in a large bowl; set aside. Combine remaining ingredients in a saucepan; bring to a boil. Pour over vegetables and toss well. Chill several hours or overnight. Yield: about 6 to 8 servings.

Buffet Beans

1 (10-3/4-ounce) can tomato soup, undiluted
1 tablespoon Worcestershire sauce
2 strips bacon, diced
6 tablespoons chopped onion
1/2 cup chopped green pepper
1/4 cup finely chopped celery
1 tablespoon prepared mustard
1/2 cup light molasses
2 (16-ounce) cans pork and beans

Combine all ingredients except pork and beans; let stand 15 minutes. Add pork and beans, mixing well. Spoon into greased 2-quart baking dish. Bake at 325° for 1-1/2 hours. Yield: 6 to 8 servings.

Marinated Vegetables

Weathervane, 1836, New-York Historical Society

6 tablespoons lemon juice
6 tablespoons vinegar
6 tablespoons olive oil
1/4 cup garlic salt
2/3 cup vegetable oil
4 teaspoons salt
1 teaspoon sugar
Dash of pepper
1/2 head cauliflower
3 stalks celery, cut into sticks
3 to 4 carrots, cut into sticks
10 to 15 cherry tomatoes, halved

Combine all ingredients except vegetables; mix well, and set aside.

Cut cauliflower flowerets 1 inch from top of stalks; then cut into bite-size pieces.

Arrange vegetables on a serving platter, and pour marinade over all. Marinate 6 hours before serving. Yield: 6 to 8 servings.

Chocolate Dreams

1 cup shortening
4 (1-ounce) squares unsweetened chocolate
2 cups sugar
4 eggs, well beaten
1 teaspoon vanilla extract
1-1/2 cups all-purpose flour
1/2 teaspoon salt
1 cup chopped pecans
Frosting (recipe follows)

Melt shortening and chocolate in top of a double boiler; add sugar, mixing well. Add eggs and vanilla; mix well. Stir in flour and salt, and mix thoroughly. Remove from heat, and stir in nuts.

Spread batter in a well-greased 13-1/2- x 8- x 3/4-inch pan. Bake at 400° for 20 minutes. Cool; spread with frosting. Yield: about 36 squares.

Frosting:
2 (1-ounce) squares unsweetened chocolate
3 tablespoons hot water
1 tablespoon butter or margarine
2 to 2-1/2 cups powdered sugar
1/2 teaspoon vanilla extract
1 egg

Melt chocolate with water, and blend in butter. Stir in powdered sugar and vanilla; beat in egg. Yield: enough frosting for 36 squares.

Butterscotch Squares

1/2 cup butter, softened
2 cups firmly packed dark brown sugar
2 eggs
2 cups all-purpose flour
2 teaspoons baking powder
1/2 teaspoon salt
1 teaspoon vanilla extract
1 cup chopped pecans
1 cup flaked coconut
1 (6-ounce) package butterscotch pieces

Cream butter and sugar until light and fluffy; add eggs, one at a time, beating well after each addition. Combine flour, baking powder, and salt; add to creamed mixture, mixing until smooth. Stir in vanilla, pecans, coconut, and butterscotch pieces.

Spread batter evenly in a lightly greased 9-inch square pan. Bake at 350° for 30 to 35 minutes. Cut into bars while warm. Yield: 25 (1-1/2-inch) bars.

Milky Way Cake

8 (1-7/8-ounce) chocolate-covered malt-caramel candy bars
1/2 cup melted butter or margarine
2 cups sugar
1/2 cup butter or margarine, softened
4 eggs
1 teaspoon vanilla extract
1-1/4 cups buttermilk
1/2 teaspoon soda
3 cups all-purpose flour
1 cup chopped pecans
Milk Chocolate Frosting

Combine candy bars and 1/2 cup melted butter in a saucepan; place over low heat until candy bars are melted, stirring constantly. Cool.

Cream sugar and 1/2 cup softened butter until light and fluffy. Add eggs, one at a time, beating well after each addition; stir in vanilla.

Combine buttermilk and soda; add to creamed mixture alternately with flour, beating well after each addition. Stir in candy bar mixture and pecans.

Pour batter into a greased and floured 10-inch tube pan; bake at 325° for 1 hour and 20 minutes or until done.

Let cool in pan 1 hour; remove from pan, and complete cooling on wire rack. Frost with Milk Chocolate Frosting. Yield: one 10-inch cake.

Milk Chocolate Frosting:
2-1/2 cups sugar
1 cup evaporated milk, undiluted
1/2 cup melted butter or margarine
1 (6-ounce) package semisweet chocolate morsels
1 cup marshmallow cream
Milk

Combine sugar, evaporated milk, and butter in a heavy saucepan; cook over medium heat until a small amount dropped in cold water forms a soft ball.

Remove from heat; add chocolate pieces and marshmallow cream, stirring until melted.

If necessary, add a small amount of milk to make spreading consistency. Yield: frosting for one 10-inch cake.

Lemon Spice Bars

1 cup all-purpose flour
1 teaspoon baking powder
1/4 teaspoon ground cinnamon
1/4 teaspoon ground nutmeg
1 cup quick-cooking oats, uncooked
1-1/3 cups firmly packed brown sugar
3/4 cup vegetable oil
2 eggs, slightly beaten
2 teaspoons lemon juice
1/2 teaspoon vanilla extract
1/2 cup chopped pecans
Lemon glaze (recipe follows)

Combine first 6 ingredients, stirring well. Add oil, eggs, flavorings, and nuts; mix thoroughly.

Spoon batter into a greased and floured 13- x 9- x 2-inch baking pan; bake at 350° for 25 minutes. Spread glaze over top while hot. Let cool, and cut into 2- x 1-inch bars. Yield: about 5 dozen.

Lemon Glaze:
1-1/2 to 2 cups powdered sugar
1 tablespoon lemon juice
1/4 teaspoon ground cinnamon
3 tablespoons milk

Combine all ingredients, mixing until smooth. Yield: about 3/4 cup.

Porters carrying a picnic hamper; from a 17th-century drawing, NYPL

Robert M. Kulicke: **Tomato,** *1978, Private Collection, Courtesy of Davis & Long Company, New York*

"The Golden Apple"

The tomato is a latecomer to the diet of Europeans—an altogether astonishing fact in view of the tomato's importance in Italian and French cooking today. Like potatoes and corn, it is a native of the New World, and was brought to Europe by the Spanish in the sixteenth century in its rather unprepossessing native form: small and yellow. "Golden apple" the Italians called it—*pomodoro*—but, apple or not, they certainly did not eat it. They grew it as an ornamental fruit, and only in the eighteenth century (by which time they had coaxed the fruit into something like its present form) did they consider it food. Thomas Jefferson was the first American to cultivate tomatoes, but even the Presidential endorsement was not enough to persuade his compatriots to follow the European example. Until the late nineteenth century, most Americans shunned tomatoes, believing them to be poisonous. Times change, and nowadays tomatoes grown and ripened in one's own garden and served quite plain have become one of the joys of summer.

Robert Kulicke's *Tomato*, opposite, is so faithfully painted that it seems scarcely a step removed from the glowing basketful in the photograph at right. And yet, strangely enough, it is not meant to fool the eye. There is nothing photographic about it. Kulicke, a painter living in New York City, belongs to the school of classic American realists that includes Raphaelle Peale, who painted the still-life on the jacket of this book. Their approach is part of a tradition also embraced by Cézanne (page 40) and the endless parade of painters who take the objects of daily life and make us see the art in them.

Garden-fresh perfection photographed by Jerome Drown

97

Tomatoes

Ahhh! . . . to bite (slowly, so as not to dribble) into a tomato ripe in its own sun is to know one of the few heavens on this earth. The explosive abundance of even the smallest planting calls for every ingenuity — soups, sauces, pies, aspics, salads, preserves — for use now or to keep this red and golden miracle for a less blessed time of year.

Grilled Italian Tomatoes

3 large firm-ripe tomatoes
2 tablespoons commercial Italian dressing
1-1/2 teaspoons basil
Salt and pepper to taste
1/4 cup melted butter or margarine
1 cup breadcrumbs

Cut tomatoes in half crosswise, and sprinkle each half with 1 teaspoon Italian dressing, 1/4 teaspoon basil, salt, and pepper. Combine butter and breadcrumbs; spoon over tomato halves.

Place tomato halves on heavy-duty aluminum foil. Seal foil, leaving a small amount of space for steam to escape. Cook over hot coals for 10 minutes. Yield: 6 servings.

Tomato 'n Honey Barbecue Sauce

1/2 cup olive oil
1 onion, chopped
1 clove garlic, minced
1/4 cup vinegar
4 to 5 tomatoes, peeled and chopped
2 teaspoons pepper
1/2 cup dark corn syrup
1/3 cup honey

Combine first 6 ingredients in a large saucepan; simmer 40 minutes. Stir in syrup and honey; simmer 20 minutes. Use on spareribs or other meat. Brush on cooked side of meat to prevent scorching. Yield: about 2 cups.

Tomato Bisque

2 (10-3/4-ounce) cans chicken broth
1-1/3 cups canned tomatoes
1 cup chopped celery
2 teaspoons chopped onion
1 cup chopped carrots
1/2 teaspoon salt
6 tablespoons butter or margarine, divided
1/4 cup all-purpose flour
2-2/3 cups half-and-half, scalded
2 large tomatoes, peeled and chopped
2 tablespoons sugar
1/2 teaspoon salt
1/4 teaspoon soda
Paprika

Combine broth, canned tomatoes, celery, onion, carrots, and 1/2 teaspoon salt in a saucepan. Heat to boiling point; reduce heat and simmer 20 minutes. Strain; reserve broth and discard the vegetables.

Melt 3 tablespoons butter in a saucepan; gradually stir in flour. Cook, stirring constantly, over low heat 2 minutes. Gradually add half-and-half, stirring constantly. Cook, stirring constantly, until thickened. Remove from heat; stir in reserved broth. Set aside and keep warm.

Melt remaining 3 tablespoons butter in a skillet. Add fresh tomato; sauté 2 to 4 minutes. Stir in sugar, remaining 1/2 teaspoon salt, and soda. Add to broth mixture, stirring well. Garnish with paprika. Yield: about 8 servings.

Tomatoes Rockefeller

12 thick slices tomato
2 (10-ounce) packages frozen chopped spinach
1 cup soft breadcrumbs
1 cup seasoned breadcrumbs
1 to 1-1/2 cups finely chopped green onion
6 eggs, slightly beaten
3/4 cup melted butter or margarine
1/2 cup grated Parmesan cheese
1/2 teaspoon minced garlic
1 teaspoon salt
1 teaspoon thyme
Hot sauce to taste

Arrange tomato slices in a lightly greased 13- x 9- x 2-inch baking dish; set aside.

Cook spinach according to package directions; drain well and squeeze to remove excess water. Add remaining ingredients, stirring well. Mound mixture on tomato slices. Bake at 350° about 15 minutes or until spinach mixture is set. Yield: 12 servings.

Stuffed Tomato Surprise

3 slices bacon
1/4 cup chopped onion
1/2 pound fresh spinach, chopped
1/2 cup commercial sour cream
Dash of hot sauce
4 medium tomatoes
Salt
1/2 cup shredded mozzarella cheese

Cook bacon until crisp; drain, reserving 2 tablespoons drippings. Crumble bacon, and set aside.

Sauté onion in reserved bacon drippings until tender; stir in spinach. Cover and cook 3 to 5 minutes or until tender. Remove from heat; stir in sour cream, bacon, and hot sauce.

Cut tops from tomatoes; scoop out pulp, leaving shells intact. Chop pulp, and add to spinach mixture. Drain tomato shells, and sprinkle with salt; fill with vegetable mixture.

Place stuffed tomatoes in an 8-inch square baking dish; bake at 375° for 20 to 25 minutes. Top with cheese, and bake an additional 3 minutes or until cheese melts. Yield: 4 servings.

Marinated Tomatoes

1/2 cup vegetable oil
2 tablespoons vinegar
2 tablespoons lemon juice
1/2 teaspoon salt
1/4 teaspoon dry mustard
4 medium tomatoes, cut into 3/4-inch slices
1 medium onion, sliced
Parsley

Combine vegetable oil, vinegar, lemon juice, salt, and mustard in a small mixing bowl, stirring well. Place tomatoes in a medium bowl; add marinade. Top with onion slices and parsley. Cover bowl, and refrigerate overnight. Yield: about 6 to 8 servings.

An exuberant American label from the collections of the Library of Congress

Everything Italian Sauce

2 pounds hot Italian sausage links, cut into small
    pieces
2 (16-ounce) cans tomatoes, chopped
2 (8-ounce) cans tomato sauce
2 (6-ounce) cans tomato paste
1 (4-ounce) can sliced mushrooms
2 cups chopped onion
1 medium-size green pepper, chopped
1 teaspoon fines herbes
2 teaspoons celery flakes
2 teaspoons garlic powder
Red pepper flakes to taste
Salt and pepper to taste
Hot cooked spaghetti (optional)

    Cook sausage until browned; drain well. Combine sausage and remaining ingredients except spaghetti in a large saucepan; simmer 4 to 6 hours, stirring occasionally. Serve over spaghetti, or use as the base for other Italian dishes. (This sauce freezes well.) Yield: about 2 quarts.

Spicy Spaghetti Sauce

1 pound ground beef
1 pound ground veal
1/2 pound ground pork
1/2 cup olive oil
2 large onions, chopped
1/2 pound mushrooms, sliced
2 cloves garlic, minced
1 (16-ounce) can tomatoes, chopped
1 (10-1/2-ounce) can tomato puree
2 cups beef broth
1/2 cup red wine
1/2 teaspoon oregano
1/2 teaspoon basil
1/4 teaspoon ground nutmeg
1/8 teaspoon rosemary
2 to 3 teaspoons pepper
1 teaspoon paprika
Salt to taste
Hot cooked spaghetti

    Brown meat in a Dutch oven; drain and remove from pan. Heat olive oil in Dutch oven. Add onion, mushrooms, and garlic; sauté 5 minutes. Add tomatoes, tomato puree, beef broth, and wine; cook 10 minutes, stirring occasionally. Add meat and seasonings, blending well. Simmer over low heat 1-1/2 hours, stirring occasionally. Let stand at least 30 minutes; skim fat off top. Serve over hot spaghetti. Yield: 8 to 10 servings.

Engraving of a tomato vine, 1633

Zippy Tomato Soup

6 cups tomato juice
1 (10-1/2-ounce) can tomato puree
3 tablespoons light brown sugar
5 whole cloves
1/8 teaspoon ground cloves
1 onion slice
2 cups consommé
1-1/4 teaspoons seasoned salt
1 bay leaf, crushed
Dash of crushed thyme
Dash of crushed marjoram
Lemon slices

    Combine all ingredients except lemon slices. Bring to a boil, stirring occasionally. Simmer 5 minutes. Garnish with lemon slices. Yield: about 8 servings.

Gazpacho

1/2 cup diced celery
1/2 cup diced green pepper
1/2 cup diced onion
1/2 cup thinly sliced cucumber
1 cup diced tomatoes
1 (10-3/4-ounce) can tomato soup, undiluted
1 soup can water
1-1/2 cups cocktail vegetable juice
1 tablespoon wine vinegar
1 tablespoon commercial Italian dressing
Garlic salt to taste
1/4 teaspoon salt
1/8 teaspoon pepper
4 dashes of hot sauce
Dash of Worcestershire sauce

    Combine all ingredients in a large bowl. Cover and refrigerate at least 4 hours. Stir gently. Serve in chilled bowls or mugs. Yield: 6 to 8 servings.

Fresh Tomato Aspic

2 envelopes unflavored gelatin
2 cups cold water, divided
2 chicken bouillon cubes
1 cup tomato juice
2 tablespoons lemon juice
2 teaspoons dillweed
1 teaspoon salt
1/2 teaspoon hot sauce
1/4 cup chopped green onion
2 cups peeled and chopped fresh tomatoes
1 cup peeled, seeded, and chopped cucumbers
Lettuce (optional)

    Soften gelatin in 1 cup cold water; add bouillon cubes. Place over low heat, stirring constantly, until gelatin and bouillon cubes dissolve. Remove from heat, and add remaining 1 cup water, tomato juice, lemon juice, dillweed, salt, hot sauce, and green onion. Chill gelatin mixture until consistency of unbeaten egg white.

    Fold tomato and cucumber into thickened gelatin, and spoon into an 8-inch square dish or a 1-quart mold. Chill until firm. Cut into squares or unmold. Serve on lettuce leaves, if desired. Yield: 6 to 8 servings.

Tomato Pie

1 unbaked 10-inch pastry shell
2 large ripe tomatoes, cut into 1/2-inch slices
Salt and pepper
All-purpose flour
2 tablespoons vegetable oil
1 cup sliced green onion
1/2 cup sliced ripe olives
3 slices provolone cheese
2 eggs, slightly beaten
1 cup shredded Cheddar cheese
1 cup evaporated milk

    Prick bottom and sides of pastry shell; bake at 350° for 8 minutes or until lightly browned. Set aside to cool.

    Sprinkle tomato slices with salt and pepper; coat both sides with flour. Sauté in hot oil until golden brown.

    Set aside 2 tablespoons onion; sprinkle remaining onion and olives in pastry shell. Top with provolone cheese and tomatoes.

    Combine eggs, Cheddar cheese, and evaporated milk; mix well, and pour over tomatoes. Bake at 375° for 40 to 45 minutes or until filling is set. Sprinkle with reserved onion, and let stand 5 minutes before cutting. Yield: 6 to 8 servings.

Pieter Brueghel: **Hunters in the Snow**, *1565, Kunsthistorisches Museum, Vienna*

Soups and Stews

No painting, or indeed photograph, has ever caught the winter light more truly than Pieter Brueghel's *Hunters in the Snow*, done in 1565. The landscape is probably Flemish, but in spite of its honest exactitude it could be almost anybody's country. All the chill grandeur of a snowy day is here: the black trees, the dull sky, the powdery valley and hills, the bundled-up figures. Finding all the action in a Brueghel is an endless game. This picture, for example, harbors a score of interior pictures. The skinny hounds dawdle behind the hunters, who bring home only a fox. A group warms itself around a bonfire in front of the inn. A blackbird wheels through the air as its companions perch in the naked branches. In the distance are churches and houses, skaters and ice-fishers, and, on the tiny bridge, a stout woman in an apron hurrying along under a heavy load of kindling. The whole heart of the village is here.

While he makes the viewer keenly feel the cold, Brueghel also makes him sense the warmth of the solid houses. Surely fires burn on every hearth, and over each fire hangs a simmering kettle, its contents perfuming the air with the promise of a soup or a stew to chase away the chill. The recipes that follow will likewise bring comfort in bitter weather. Some are Southern (among them, the rich seafood gumbo at right), others European (Irish stew, onion soup), and one—Brunswick stew—is American Indian. When winter comes, can soup be far behind?

Seafood Gumbo photographed by Jerome Drown

101

Soups and Stews

Be it Kentucky Burgoo, Texas Chili, or a Bayou Country Gumbo, each region of the South offers its own robust soup or stew to warm and satisfy.

Oyster and Spinach Soup

1/2 cup finely chopped onion
2 cloves garlic, minced (optional)
1/2 cup melted butter
3 (12-ounce) cans oysters, drained and chopped
1/2 cup all-purpose flour
1-1/2 quarts half-and-half or milk
2 cups chicken broth
2 (10-ounce) packages frozen spinach, thawed and pureed
1 tablespoon salt
White pepper to taste

Sauté onion and garlic in butter until tender; add oysters, and cook until edges begin to curl. Blend in flour, and cook until bubbly. Gradually add half-and-half; cook, stirring constantly, until thickened. Stir in broth and spinach; bring to a boil. Remove from heat, and season with salt and pepper. Yield: 8 to 10 servings.

Salmon Stew

1 quart milk
1/2 cup butter or margarine
1 (16-ounce) can salmon, drained, bones removed, and flaked
1/2 cup milk
1/4 cup all-purpose flour
Salt and pepper to taste

Combine 1 quart milk and butter in a Dutch oven; place over medium heat until butter melts. Stir in salmon.

Combine 1/2 cup milk and flour, blending until smooth; add to salmon mixture, stirring well. Bring to a boil; lower heat. Add salt and pepper; simmer 5 minutes. Yield: 4 to 6 servings.

Creamy Crab Soup

2 cups milk
1/4 teaspoon ground mace
1/4 teaspoon dry mustard
1/8 teaspoon ground nutmeg
2 teaspoons grated lemon peel
1 pound crabmeat
2 cups half-and-half
3 tablespoons butter or margarine
1/2 teaspoon salt
1/2 cup dry white wine
1/4 cup cracker crumbs

Combine milk, spices, and lemon peel in top of a large double boiler; stir well. Cook mixture over simmering water 10 minutes.

Stir crabmeat, half-and-half, butter, and salt into hot mixture; cook over boiling water 20 minutes, stirring often. Stir in wine and cracker crumbs. Serve immediately. Yield: 4 to 6 servings.

Shrimp Bisque

2 pounds raw shrimp, peeled and chopped
1/4 cup chopped mushrooms
2 tablespoons chopped onion
2 tablespoons chopped celery
1 tablespoon chopped carrot
3 tablespoons melted butter or margarine
Salt to taste
Cayenne pepper to taste
2 cups chicken broth
1-1/2 cups half-and-half
1/2 cup dry white wine

Sauté shrimp and vegetables in butter over low heat about 2 minutes. Stir in salt, cayenne, and chicken broth; bring to a boil, and cook 20 minutes.

Pour shrimp mixture into container of electric blender; blend until smooth. Combine shrimp puree, half-and-half, and wine in a saucepan; heat thoroughly. Serve immediately. Yield: about 6 servings.

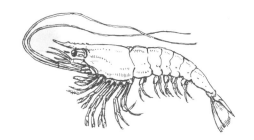

Seafood Gumbo

1 cup salad oil or bacon drippings
1 cup all-purpose flour
2 large onions, chopped
2 stalks celery, chopped
1 large green pepper, chopped
6 cloves garlic, minced
1 gallon warm water
4 cups sliced okra
3 tomatoes, peeled and chopped
2 tablespoons salt
Red and black pepper to taste
1 pint oysters, undrained
1 dozen cleaned fresh crabs* with claws or 1 pound fresh or frozen crabmeat
1-1/2 to 2 pounds fresh or frozen medium shrimp, peeled and deveined
1/2 cup chopped parsley
1/2 cup chopped green onion tops
Hot cooked rice
Gumbo filé (optional)

Combine oil and flour in a heavy pot over medium heat; cook, stirring constantly, until roux is the color of a copper penny (about 10 to 15 minutes). Add onion, celery, green pepper, and garlic to roux; cook, stirring constantly, until vegetables are tender. *Do not let roux burn* as it will ruin gumbo; reduce heat, if necessary.

Gradually add 1 gallon warm water to roux, in small amounts at first, blending well after each addition; add okra and tomatoes. Bring mixture to a boil. Reduce heat; simmer, stirring occasionally, at least 20 minutes (1 to 1-1/2 hours is better as the roux develops more flavor at this point). Stir in salt, pepper, and seafood.

Bring gumbo to a boil, and simmer 10 minutes. Add parsley and green onion; simmer 5 minutes longer. Remove from heat, and serve the gumbo over hot rice.

Gumbo can be further thickened, if desired, by adding a small amount of filé to each serving. Yield: 12 to 14 servings.

*To clean fresh crabs: Pour scalding water over crabs to kill them; remove large claws, and wash thoroughly. Turn crab upside down and lift the long, tapered point (the apron); pull off shell and remove the soft, spongy mass. Remove and discard legs. Wash crab thoroughly, and break body in half lengthwise; add to gumbo along with claws.

Note: Almost any kind of meat, poultry, or game can be substituted for the seafood in this recipe. Just cut it into pieces and brown it before adding to the roux.

Georgia Brunswick Stew

2-1/2 pounds chicken pieces, skinned and diced
2 quarts water, divided
1 cup finely chopped carrots
1 cup finely chopped celery
1 cup finely chopped onion
1 cup green peas
1 cup whole kernel corn
1/2 cup cut asparagus
1/2 cup half-and-half
1/2 cup plus 2 tablespoons all-purpose flour
2 tablespoons salt
1 tablespoon pepper
1 tablespoon chicken bouillon granules
1 pimiento, chopped

Combine chicken and 1 quart water; simmer 35 to 45 minutes or until thoroughly cooked. Drain and set aside.

In another saucepan, combine 1 quart water, carrots, celery, and onion; cover and simmer until barely tender. Add peas, corn, and asparagus; cook until tender.

Make a roux of half-and-half and flour; gradually add to vegetables, stirring constantly. Add salt, pepper, bouillon granules, pimiento, and chicken; simmer 15 minutes. Yield: 8 to 10 servings.

Texas Championship Chili

2 large onions, chopped
3 cloves garlic, minced
1 jalapeño pepper, finely chopped
1 tablespoon peanut oil
3 pounds boneless chuck roast, finely diced
1 teaspoon cumin seeds
1-1/2 tablespoons oregano
1 (1-1/2-ounce) can chili powder
1 (28-ounce) can whole tomatoes
3-1/2 cups water
1-1/2 teaspoons instant corn masa (optional)
Shredded Cheddar cheese (optional)

Sauté onion, garlic, and jalapeño pepper in oil until tender; set aside. Combine meat, cumin, and oregano in a Dutch oven; cook until meat is browned. Add onion mixture, chili powder, tomatoes, and water; bring to a boil. Reduce heat and simmer 2 to 3 hours; stirring frequently.

For thicker chili, combine corn masa with small amount of cold water to make a paste; add to chili, stirring constantly. Top with shredded cheese, if desired. Yield: 5 to 7 servings.

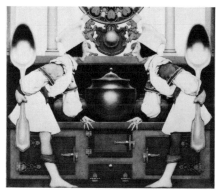

Two cooks by Maxfield Parrish

Kentucky Burgoo

1 (4- to 5-pound) hen
1 pound beef stew meat
1 pound veal stew meat
1-1/2 to 2 pounds beef or knuckle bones
1 stalk celery
1 carrot, peeled
1 small onion, peeled
5 to 6 sprigs parsley
1 (10-1/2-ounce) can tomato puree
4 quarts water
1 red pepper pod
3 tablespoons salt
1 tablespoon lemon juice
1 tablespoon Worcestershire sauce
1 tablespoon sugar
1-1/2 teaspoons black pepper
1/2 teaspoon cayenne
6 onions, finely chopped
8 to 10 tomatoes, peeled and chopped
1 turnip, peeled and finely chopped
2 green peppers, finely chopped
2 cups fresh butterbeans
2 cups thinly sliced celery
2 cups finely chopped cabbage
2 cups sliced fresh okra
2 cups fresh corn (3 to 4 ears)
1/2 unpeeled lemon, seeded

Combine first 17 ingredients in a large pot; bring to a boil. Cover and simmer 4 hours; cool. Strain meat mixture, reserving meat and stock; discard vegetables. Remove bone, skin, and gristle from meat; finely chop meat. Return meat to stock and refrigerate overnight.

The next day, remove fat layer on stock. Add remaining ingredients; cover and simmer 1 hour. Uncover and simmer about 2 hours longer, stirring frequently to prevent sticking. Burgoo is ready when it reaches the consistency of a thick stew. Yield: about 1 gallon.

Chuckwagon Stew

1 teaspoon sugar
1/4 cup all-purpose flour
2 pounds lean beef for stewing, cut into 1-inch cubes
2 tablespoons melted shortening
2 teaspoons salt
1/4 teaspoon pepper
1 teaspoon chili powder
1/4 teaspoon thyme
1 bay leaf
2 tomatoes, peeled and quartered
1 (10-1/2-ounce) can beef broth
6 small potatoes, peeled and quartered
6 small carrots, cut into 2-inch pieces
6 small whole onions, peeled
3 or 4 stalks celery, cut into 2-inch pieces
1 cup frozen green peas

Combine sugar and flour. Coat beef with flour mixture, and brown in hot shortening.

Add seasonings, tomatoes, and broth to meat; cover and simmer over low heat about 1-1/2 to 2 hours or until meat is almost tender. Stir in vegetables except peas; cover and cook about 30 minutes. Add peas; cover and cook about 15 more minutes. Yield: 6 to 8 servings.

Irish Stew

1 pound lean lamb, cut into 1-1/2-inch cubes
Salt
Pepper
About 1/4 cup all-purpose flour
2 to 4 tablespoons salad oil
1 onion, sliced
2 cups boiling water
4 small carrots, sliced
2 potatoes, diced
1 turnip, diced
1 tablespoon chopped parsley

Season meat generously with salt and pepper; sprinkle with flour. Heat salad oil in a Dutch oven over medium heat. Add meat and onion; sauté until browned, stirring occasionally. Stir in boiling water; cover and simmer about 1 hour or until meat is tender, stirring occasionally.

Add carrots, potatoes, and turnip to meat mixture, and cook 20 minutes longer or until vegetables are tender. Stir in parsley before serving. Yield: 4 to 6 servings.

Charles Demuth: Still Life with Eggplant and Summer Squash, *1927, Wadsworth Atheneum*

Squash–American Native

"Squash" is an Indian word, and, like corn, squash was an essential crop for the Indians: it has been eaten in the Western Hemisphere for as long as there have been people to eat it. Squash, corn, and beans were the vegetable triad that kept the inhabitants of the New World well nourished long before the Europeans arrived. The variety of squash is almost magical: hubbard and acorn, crooknecks, pattypans, zucchini, pumpkins, butternuts. Depending on the time of year and the kind, squash can be eaten raw, baked, boiled, or fried; many make excellent pies. They combine readily with onions, tomatoes, mushrooms, cheese, or meat. They are easy to grow, they keep well, and because most of them are naturally packaged in a durable skin, they lose none of their goodness on the trip from garden to market to table.

Of all vegetables, perhaps, squash have the most sculptural forms. String beans, peas, and Brussels sprouts may taste delicious, but the dark-green furrows of a hubbard, still handsome after the squash is baked, or the alabaster scallops of a pattypan squash (also known as summer squash or cymling) are minor works of abstract art in themselves. The summer squash opposite, accompanied by an eggplant, are the work of Charles Demuth, a talented but not widely known painter and watercolorist, one of the American expatriates in the circle of Gertrude Stein, Picasso, and Hemingway in Paris during the 1920s.

Stuffed zucchini and yellow squash
photographed by Jerome Drown

105

Squash

Squash is a vegetable for all seasons—a versatile and varied species with a long productive period and good tolerance for storage. Traditionally a Southern vegetable, squash may be prepared in a great variety of ways.

Tangy Yellow Squash

5 medium-size yellow squash, thinly sliced
1/2 cup thinly sliced green onion
1/2 cup chopped green pepper
1/2 cup sliced celery
2 tablespoons wine vinegar
3/4 cup sugar
1 teaspoon salt
1/2 teaspoon pepper
1/3 cup vegetable oil
2/3 cup cider vinegar
1 clove garlic, crushed

Combine squash, green onion, green pepper, and celery in a large mixing bowl; toss lightly. Combine wine vinegar, sugar, salt, pepper, salad oil, cider vinegar, and garlic; stir well and spoon over vegetables. Chill about 12 hours, stirring occasionally. Drain and serve. Yield: 10 servings.

Zucchini-Tomato Kabobs

1/2 pound fresh mushrooms
1-1/2 pounds small zucchini, cut into 1-inch slices
12 to 18 large cherry tomatoes
Commercial Italian salad dressing
9 (1-inch) fresh pineapple chunks

Clean mushrooms with a damp cloth; remove stems. Combine mushrooms, zucchini, tomatoes, and salad dressing; cover and marinate in refrigerator 4 hours or overnight.

Drain vegetables, and reserve marinade; thread vegetables alternately with pineapple onto 3 long skewers. Cook on grill over medium heat 10 minutes, turning occasionally and basting frequently with reserved marinade. Yield: 6 servings.

Spinach-Stuffed Zucchini

3 medium zucchini
Salt to taste
1 (10-ounce) package frozen chopped spinach
2 tablespoons all-purpose flour
1/2 cup milk
4 slices bacon, cooked, drained, and crumbled
1/3 cup shredded Cheddar cheese
Chopped pimiento (optional)

Wash zucchini thoroughly; cut off stem end. Drop zucchini into a small amount of boiling salted water; cover, lower heat, and cook 10 to 12 minutes. Drain, and allow to cool to touch.

Cut zucchini in half lengthwise; remove pulp, leaving a firm shell; chop pulp. Sprinkle shells with salt to taste; set aside.

Cook spinach according to package directions; drain, and squeeze dry. Combine flour and milk; add zucchini pulp and spinach. Cook over low heat, stirring constantly, until thickened. Spoon spinach mixture into zucchini shells; sprinkle with bacon, then with cheese.

Place zucchini shells in a shallow baking pan; bake at 350° for 15 to 20 minutes. Garnish with pimiento, if desired. Yield: 6 servings.

Green and Gold Squash Pie

1 unbaked 10-inch pastry shell
2 medium zucchini, thinly sliced
2 medium-size yellow squash, thinly sliced
1/2 medium onion, chopped
2 green onions, sliced
1 large clove garlic, minced
1 medium tomato, peeled and chopped
1 medium-size green pepper, finely chopped
3/4 teaspoon salt
1/4 teaspoon pepper
1/2 teaspoon basil
2 tablespoons melted butter or margarine
3 eggs, beaten
1/2 cup whipping cream
1/4 cup grated Parmesan cheese

Prick bottom and sides of pastry shell; bake at 450° for 8 minutes or until lightly browned. Set aside to cool.

Combine vegetables, salt, pepper, basil, and butter in a large skillet; sauté until vegetables are tender. Spoon into pastry shell, spreading evenly. Combine eggs and cream, mixing well; pour over vegetables. Sprinkle with cheese, and bake at 350° for 30 minutes or until set. Yield: 6 to 8 servings.

Butternut Soufflé

2 cups cooked, mashed butternut squash
3 tablespoons margarine
1 cup sugar or 3/4 cup honey
1/3 cup milk
1/2 teaspoon salt
1 teaspoon ground cinnamon
1/2 teaspoon ground nutmeg
3 eggs
1 teaspoon vanilla extract

Combine squash and margarine, mixing well. Add sugar, milk, salt, and spices; mix thoroughly. Add eggs, beating well. Stir in vanilla.

Pour mixture into a greased 1-1/2-quart casserole. Bake at 325° for 1 hour and 15 minutes or until set. Yield: 6 to 8 servings.

Zucchini French Fries

3 large zucchini, washed, peeled, and cut into (3- x 1/2- x 1/2-inch) strips
All-purpose flour
Salad oil
Salt
Catsup (optional)

Coat all sides of squash strips with flour; fry until lightly browned in 1 inch of oil heated to 375°. Drain; sprinkle with salt. Serve with catsup, if desired. Yield: 4 to 6 servings.

Zucchini Bread

1 cup salad oil
3 eggs, slightly beaten
2 cups sugar
2 cups grated raw zucchini
2 teaspoons vanilla extract
3 cups all-purpose flour
1 teaspoon soda
1/4 teaspoon baking powder
1 teaspoon salt
3 teaspoons ground cinnamon
1 cup chopped walnuts or pecans

Combine oil, eggs, sugar, zucchini, and vanilla in a large mixing bowl; blend well. Stir in flour, soda, baking powder, salt, and cinnamon. Do not beat. Stir in walnuts.

Spoon batter into 2 well-greased 8-1/2- x 4-1/2- x 2-5/8-inch loafpans. Bake at 325° for 1-1/2 hours or until done. Yield: 2 loaves.

Squash Fritters

2 cups cooked, mashed yellow squash
2 eggs, beaten
1 small onion, chopped
Salt and pepper to taste
1/2 cup cracker crumbs
Hot salad oil

Combine squash, eggs, onion, seasonings, and cracker crumbs; mix well. Drop mixture by tablespoonfuls into hot oil; cook until golden brown, turning once. Yield: 6 servings.

Baked Acorn Squash

2 medium acorn squash
Butter or margarine
Lemon juice
4 teaspoons butter or margarine
4 tablespoons brown sugar
Ground coriander

Cut squash in half; scoop out seeds. Spread butter over cut edges. Place cut side down in a greased baking dish. Bake at 400° for 30 to 40 minutes or until tender.

Turn cut side up; brush with lemon juice. Place 1 teaspoon butter in each cavity. Sprinkle 1 tablespoon brown sugar over each squash half; sprinkle with coriander. Return to oven and bake about 5 minutes or until sugar has melted. Yield: 4 servings.

Zucchini-Tomato Salad

6 small zucchini, thinly sliced
4 tomatoes, cut into wedges
1 green pepper, thinly sliced into rings
1/4 cup chopped green onion
1/4 cup vinegar
1/2 teaspoon salt
1/2 teaspoon garlic salt
1/2 teaspoon pepper
3/4 cup salad oil
Lettuce (optional)

Combine zucchini, tomatoes, green pepper, and green onion; toss lightly. Combine vinegar, salt, garlic salt, pepper, and salad oil; mix well, and pour over vegetables. Chill several hours, stirring occasionally. Serve on lettuce, if desired. Yield: 6 to 8 servings.

Herb-Stuffed Pattypan Squash

6 medium pattypan squash
1 cup herb stuffing mix
1/2 cup melted butter or margarine
1/2 cup chopped green pepper
1/3 cup minced onion
1/2 teaspoon salt
Pepper to taste
Shredded Cheddar cheese (optional)

Wash squash thoroughly. Drop in boiling salted water; cover, lower heat, and cook 15 minutes or until tender but firm. Drain, and allow to cool to touch.

Place squash, flatter side down, on a smooth surface; scoop out pulp, leaving a 1/4-inch shell. Chop pulp; combine pulp and remaining ingredients except cheese, stirring well.

Spoon stuffing mixture into shells; sprinkle with cheese, if desired. Place squash in a shallow baking pan; to prevent sticking, pour in enough water to cover bottom of pan. Bake at 350° for 15 to 20 minutes. Yield: 6 servings.

Baked Butternut Squash

1 large butternut squash
1 cup water
6 tablespoons butter or margarine, divided
2 tablespoons brown sugar
1/2 teaspoon salt
1/2 teaspoon ground ginger
1 medium orange, halved
Additional ginger

Cut squash in half lengthwise; remove seeds. Place cut side down in a large baking dish. Add 1 cup water; bake at 350° for 30 minutes. Turn squash cut side up; add more water if necessary to cover bottom of pan.

Spread 1 tablespoon butter over neck of each squash half; place 1 tablespoon butter in cavity of each. Bake 30 to 45 minutes.

Scoop pulp from shell. Combine pulp, 2 tablespoons butter, brown sugar, salt, and 1/2 teaspoon ginger in a mixing bowl; beat with an electric mixer until smooth. Squeeze juice from half of orange; stir into squash mixture.

Spoon squash into a buttered 1-1/2-quart casserole. Slice remaining orange half; place on squash. Sprinkle lightly with additional ginger. Bake at 350° about 15 minutes or until hot. Yield: about 6 to 8 servings.

Delightful Squash Casserole

8 medium-size yellow squash
4 slices bacon
1 small onion, chopped
2 eggs, beaten
1 cup shredded sharp Cheddar cheese
Salt and pepper to taste
1 tablespoon Worcestershire sauce

Cook squash in a small amount of boiling salted water until tender; drain well, and mash. Cook bacon until crisp; drain well and crumble, reserving drippings. Sauté onion in reserved drippings.

Combine all ingredients, stirring well; spoon into a lightly greased 1-quart casserole. Bake at 350° for 30 minutes. Yield: 4 to 6 servings.

Detail of a market scene by Pieter Aertsen. Hailwylska Museum, Stockholm

Zesty Vegetable Tray

2 new potatoes, cooked and sliced
3 medium-size yellow squash, sliced
3 hard-cooked eggs, sliced
1 medium cucumber, sliced
3 medium tomatoes, sliced
Salt and freshly ground pepper to taste
1 to 2 cloves garlic, minced
Chopped parsley
1/3 cup vinegar
2/3 cup peanut oil
Parsley

Arrange vegetables in alternate rows on a tray; season with salt and pepper. Sprinkle with garlic and chopped parsley. Combine vinegar and oil in a jar; tighten lid securely, and shake well. Pour over vegetables. Garnish with parsley. Yield: 8 servings.

Rice

At Charleston, an old South Carolina saying goes, two rivers join to form the Atlantic Ocean. What built the culture of Colonial Charleston (in those days the only seaport of any size south of Philadelphia) and was the basis of its almost legendary self-esteem was chiefly rice. Rice grew well in the swamps and estuaries of the Tidewater. All that was needed was cheap labor, and slaves imported from Africa and the West Indies supplied that. "The Planters here all get rich," reported a Charlestonian in 1765, "which you need not wonder at when you see this small province export about 120,000 barrels of Rice. . . ." In the year 1730, there may have been no more than two thousand rice planters, but, according to modern historians, they had a higher income per capita than any other comparable group of their day.

The cultivation of rice was still a very profitable business a century later when this painting of a snowy egret in a rice paddy was made near Charleston by the famed ornithologist John James Audubon. His four hundred and thirty-five paintings of American birds, done over a seventeen-year period, have been called "one of the great individual projects of the nineteenth century," and in 1832 Audubon visited Charleston. Every spring, the egrets migrated in the thousands to South Carolina, and strutted in full plumage through the rice fields.

Rice is no longer a way to get rich quick, but it is, as it always has been, a dependably good accompaniment to sauce-y things, as the dishes in the photograph at right.

Okra Shrimp Creole, Rice Pudding with Marmalade, and Polynesian Rice Salad photographed by Taylor Lewis

109

Rice

This staple from Southern lowlands is the basis for some of the higher reaches of Southern cooking.

Cornish Hens with Orange Rice

6 Cornish hens
1 cup melted butter or margarine
1 cup apple jelly
1/4 cup cornstarch
1-1/3 cups Sauterne
1/2 cup orange juice
Salt to taste
2 cups white seedless grapes
Orange Rice

Brown hens in butter; remove from skillet, and place in a baking dish. Melt apple jelly over low heat; set aside. Add cornstarch to drippings in skillet, blending well; stir in apple jelly, Sauterne, orange juice, and salt. Cook, stirring constantly, until smooth and thickened.

Pour sauce over hens; bake, uncovered, at 350° for 1 hour. Add grapes, and bake about 10 additional minutes or until grapes are warm.

Arrange hens and Orange Rice on platter; garnish with grapes. Serve sauce with hens. Yield: 6 servings.

Orange Rice:
2 cups diced celery and leaves
6 tablespoons chopped onion
1/2 cup melted butter or margarine
2 cups uncooked regular rice
1 teaspoon salt
2-1/2 cups boiling water
1-1/2 cups orange juice
1/4 cup grated orange rind

Sauté celery and onion in butter until tender. Stir rice and salt into boiling water; cover and simmer 15 to 17 minutes. Add orange juice, orange rind, and sautéed vegetables. Cover; cook 5 minutes or until tender. Yield: 6 servings.

Risotto Parmigiana

1/2 pound chicken livers, quartered
1/2 cup chopped onion
1/2 cup melted butter or margarine, divided
3 cups uncooked regular rice
3-1/2 to 4 cups hot chicken broth
Salt and pepper to taste
1-1/2 cups grated Parmesan cheese

Sauté chicken livers and onion in 1/4 cup butter; add rice and cook 5 minutes, stirring constantly. Add chicken broth, salt, and pepper; simmer about 20 minutes or until rice is tender and all liquid is absorbed. Stir in remaining butter and Parmesan cheese. Yield: 6 servings.

Polynesian Rice Salad

1 cup long grain rice, uncooked
1/2 cup vegetable oil
1/4 cup cider vinegar
2 tablespoons soy sauce
1/2 teaspoon salt
1 cup thinly sliced celery
1/4 cup thinly sliced green onion tops
1 (8-1/2-ounce) can water chestnuts, drained and sliced
1 cup sliced fresh mushrooms
1 (11-ounce) can mandarin oranges, drained
Lettuce (optional)

Cook rice according to package directions; let cool to room temperature. Combine vegetable oil, vinegar, soy sauce, salt, celery, and onion; stir in rice. Fold in water chestnuts, mushrooms, and oranges just until blended. Chill thoroughly, and serve in a lettuce-lined bowl. Yield: 6 servings.

Mushroom Rice

1 cup uncooked regular rice
2 (4-ounce) cans sliced mushrooms, undrained
1 (10-1/2-ounce) can beef broth
2 tablespoons sherry
1/4 teaspoon salt
1/8 teaspoon garlic powder
1/8 teaspoon seasoned pepper
1/2 cup melted butter or margarine

Combine all ingredients in a 1-1/2-quart casserole. Bake, uncovered, at 350° for 1 hour. Yield: 6 servings.

Wild and Dirty Rice

1 cup chopped celery
3/4 cup chopped green pepper
3 cloves garlic, minced
3 tablespoons chopped parsley
5 green onions, chopped
1 large onion, chopped
1/2 cup olive oil
1-3/4 cups wild rice, uncooked
1/4 cup long grain rice
2 (4-ounce) cans sliced mushrooms, drained
4 cups hot chicken broth
1-1/2 cups finely chopped cooked chicken giblets
1 cup finely chopped cooked chicken
1/2 cup slivered almonds, toasted
1 tablespoon salt
1 teaspoon black pepper
1/4 teaspoon cayenne pepper
1/2 teaspoon poultry seasoning

Sauté vegetables in olive oil until tender; add remaining ingredients. Pour into a lightly greased 3-quart casserole. Cover and bake at 250° for 1 hour and 15 minutes. Yield: 8 to 10 servings.

Shrimp with Wild Rice

1/2 cup all-purpose flour
1 cup melted butter or margarine, divided
4 cups chicken broth
1/4 teaspoon white pepper
1 cup thinly sliced onion
1/2 cup thinly sliced green pepper
1 cup thinly sliced mushrooms
2 pounds cooked, peeled, deveined shrimp
2 tablespoons Worcestershire sauce
Few drops of hot sauce
4 cups cooked wild rice

Gradually add flour to 1/2 cup melted butter; cook over low heat, stirring constantly, until bubbly. Gradually add broth; cook until smooth and thickened, stirring constantly. Add white pepper; simmer 2 to 3 minutes.

Sauté onion, green pepper, and mushrooms in remaining 1/2 cup butter; drain. Combine white sauce, sautéed vegetables, and remaining ingredients; spoon into 2 greased, shallow 2-quart casseroles. Bake at 300° for 45 to 50 minutes or until bubbly. Yield: 12 servings.

Fancy Rice

1 (8-ounce) can crushed pineapple
2/3 cup instant rice
2/3 cup water
1/2 teaspoon salt
1-1/2 cups miniature marshmallows
1 banana, diced
2 teaspoons lemon juice
1 cup whipping cream, whipped

Drain pineapple, reserving juice. Combine rice, water, pineapple juice, and salt in a saucepan. Bring to a boil; then reduce heat. Cover and simmer for 5 minutes; remove from heat, and let stand 5 minutes. Stir in pineapple, marshmallows, banana, and lemon juice; cool. Fold in whipped cream. Chill. Yield: 6 to 8 servings.

Rice Pudding with Marmalade Sauce

6 cups milk
1 cup short grain rice, uncooked
1/2 teaspoon salt
1 cup sugar
3 eggs, beaten
1/4 cup butter or margarine
1 teaspoon vanilla extract
Marmalade Sauce

Bring milk to a boil in a 3-quart saucepan; add rice and salt, stirring until milk returns to a boil. Cover saucepan and reduce heat; simmer about 50 minutes. Stir in sugar.

Spoon a small amount of hot mixture into beaten eggs, and mix well. Add egg mixture to mixture in saucepan, stirring constantly; cook and stir about 5 minutes longer, and remove from heat. Stir in butter and vanilla, blending well.

Spoon pudding into a buttered 1-quart mold and refrigerate overnight, or spoon into custard cups and serve warm or cold. Top with Marmalade Sauce. Yield: 8 servings.

Marmalade Sauce:
1 teaspoon cornstarch
1/3 cup cream sherry
1 cup orange marmalade
1/4 cup chopped nuts

Dissolve cornstarch in sherry in a small saucepan; stir in marmalade and nuts. Cook over low heat, stirring constantly, just until hot. Yield: 1-1/2 cups.

Planting, *from* The Cycle of Rice. *Victoria and Albert Museum*

Shrimp and Rice Salad

1 pound shrimp, cooked, peeled, and deveined
2 cups cooked rice
1/4 cup thinly sliced celery
1/4 cup sliced stuffed olives
1/4 cup chopped green pepper
1/4 cup chopped pimiento
1/4 cup minced onion
1/2 teaspoon salt
1/4 teaspoon pepper
3 tablespoons mayonnaise or salad dressing
Lettuce
2 tomatoes, cut in wedges
Celery leaves
Commercial French dressing

Combine first 10 ingredients, and toss lightly. Chill thoroughly. Serve on lettuce, and garnish with tomato wedges and celery leaves. Serve with French dressing. Yield: 4 servings.

Cheese-Rice Cakes

1 cup cottage cheese, sieved
1 egg, slightly beaten
1/2 cup milk
1 cup cooked rice
1 tablespoon prepared mustard
1/2 cup all-purpose flour
1/2 teaspoon baking powder
1/4 teaspoon salt
1/2 cup drained whole kernel corn
Mint jelly

Combine cottage cheese and egg; stir in milk, rice, and mustard. Combine flour, baking powder, and salt. Add to cottage cheese mixture; stir until smooth. Stir in corn.

Drop by heaping tablespoonfuls onto a hot, greased griddle; cook until brown on both sides. Serve with mint jelly. Yield: 2 dozen.

Okra Shrimp Creole

3/4 cup chopped green pepper
1 cup diced celery
1 large onion, chopped
1/2 cup melted butter or margarine
1/2 teaspoon sugar
2 teaspoons salt
1/4 teaspoon hot sauce
1/4 teaspoon black pepper
1/4 teaspoon cayenne pepper
2 teaspoons Worcestershire sauce
2 tablespoons all-purpose flour
1 cup water
1 cup tomato sauce
1 (12-ounce) can cocktail vegetable juice
1 (16-ounce) can okra and tomatoes
1 (8-ounce) can tomatoes, pureed
2 pounds shrimp, peeled and deveined
1/2 cup sliced water chestnuts
Hot cooked rice
Parsley

Sauté green pepper, celery, and onion in butter. Add seasonings and flour, blending well. Stir in water, tomato sauce, vegetable juice, okra and tomatoes, and pureed tomatoes; simmer 20 minutes.

Stir in shrimp and water chestnuts, and simmer 10 to 15 minutes longer. Serve over rice, and garnish with parsley. Yield: 8 to 10 servings.

Chinese Beef and Rice

1 tablespoon vegetable oil
1/3 cup long grain rice, uncooked
3/4 cup boiling water
1/2 teaspoon beef-flavor bouillon granules
1-1/2 teaspoons soy sauce
3/4 teaspoon salt
Dash of pepper
1 small onion, chopped
1 rib celery, chopped
1 small green pepper, chopped
3/4 cup cooked, diced beef

Heat oil over medium heat; add rice, and cook until golden brown, stirring occasionally. Combine water, bouillon, soy sauce, salt, and pepper; stir into rice. Cover; lower heat, and simmer 20 minutes.

Add remaining ingredients. Cover, and simmer 10 minutes or until liquid has been absorbed. Yield: 2 servings.

Sandro Botticelli: **Primavera** *(Spring), 1478, Uffizi Gallery, Florence*

The Flavor of Spring

Botticelli's *Primavera* is a work of art that somehow stumps the experts. Generations of art scholars have tried, with arguable success, to decode its meaning. Undoubtedly one of the most beautiful creations of the Italian Renaissance, it depicts a group of mythic creatures, all young and handsome, cavorting in the woods. It must be spring, for the grass is teeming with flowers: forty different species can be discerned, including cabbage roses, English daisies, violets, daffodils, and grape hyacinths. And the trees are bursting with bloom, though, oddly enough, ripe fruit hangs on them as well. At the center of the group is an elegantly dressed woman identified as Venus (although Venus is traditionally portrayed nude). On her right, the Three Graces dance in a ring while a young man—presumably the god Mercury—examines the fruit above his head. To her left is a woman carrying flowers and clad in a filmy print gown that would be the height of style today. Beside her is a scantily dressed nymph in the clutches of a fierce creature usually thought to be Zephyr, the wind god. Despite all this activity, nothing could be calmer, gentler, or more sedate than this scene. The best solution to the mystery may be simply to accept the picture and enjoy it for what it is, as we might accept the bowl of strawberries at right, and other gifts of spring.

Strawberries being washed, photographed by Phillip Kretchmar

Spring

In the Spring the good cook's fancy lightly turns to thoughts of tender asparagus, plump strawberries, and young lamb.

Strawberry Soup

2 cups strawberries, hulled and crushed
2 tablespoons lemon juice
3 cups water
1 cup sugar
2 tablespoons quick-cooking tapioca
1 cup sweet white wine

Combine strawberries, lemon juice, water, sugar, and tapioca in a medium saucepan; mix well. Bring to a boil over medium heat, stirring often, and cook 15 minutes. Stir in wine; chill. Yield: about 5-1/2 cups.

Strawberry Meringue Tarts

3 egg whites (at room temperature)
1/2 teaspoon almond extract
1/2 teaspoon cream of tartar
Dash of salt
1 cup sugar, sifted
About 1 cup commercial sour cream
Whole strawberries

Combine egg whites, almond extract, cream of tartar, and salt; beat until frothy. Gradually add sugar, 1 tablespoon at a time, beating until glossy and stiff peaks form. Do not underbeat.

Drop meringue by tablespoonfuls onto a cookie sheet that has been covered with heavy brown paper. Using back of a small spoon, make a small depression in top of each meringue. Bake at 250° about 30 minutes. Turn off oven; leave meringues in oven with the door closed 1 hour for a crisper meringue.

Cool meringues away from drafts. Place 1 teaspoon sour cream in each meringue; top each with a whole strawberry. Yield: about 40.

Artichokes Primavera

4 medium artichokes
Lemon slices
Salt
4 teaspoons vegetable oil
2 cups diced carrots
2 tablespoons melted butter
3/4 teaspoon sugar
1/2 cup water
1/3 cup half-and-half
3 egg yolks
1 to 2 teaspoons lemon juice

Wash artichokes well, and trim stem even with base. Slice about 3/4 inch off top of artichoke, and remove discolored leaves at base. Trim off thorny leaf tips.

Tie string around each artichoke from top to bottom to hold leaves in place during cooking. (If not cooking immediately, place artichokes in a bowl containing 1 tablespoon lemon juice to 1 quart water to prevent discoloration.)

Place artichokes in 2 inches water in a deep saucepan. Add a few lemon slices, salt, and vegetable oil. Cover and cook over medium heat 25 to 40 minutes or until leaves pull out easily.

Remove artichokes from water using tongs; place upside down to drain. Untie string, and gently spread center leaves apart; pull out center leaves, and scrape off the fuzzy thistle center (choke) with a spoon.

Sauté carrots in butter about 5 minutes; add 3/4 teaspoon salt, sugar, and 1/2 cup water. Cover and simmer 10 to 15 minutes or until carrots are tender. Do not drain.

Combine half-and-half and egg yolks; beat well. Add egg yolk mixture to carrots; cook over low heat, stirring constantly, until slightly thickened. Stir in lemon juice. Spoon carrot mixture into center of each artichoke. Serve immediately. Yield: 4 servings.

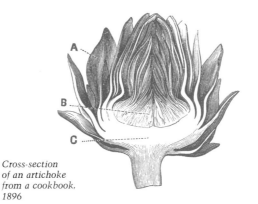

Cross-section of an artichoke from a cookbook, 1896

Asparagus with Egg Sauce

2 to 2-1/2 pounds fresh asparagus
3 tablespoons butter or margarine
3 tablespoons all-purpose flour
1 teaspoon salt
2 cups milk
Dash of Worcestershire sauce
1 teaspoon lemon juice
1/4 teaspoon onion juice
4 hard-cooked eggs, chopped
Lemon
Pimiento strips
Parsley

Cook asparagus in a small amount of boiling salted water 12 to 15 minutes or until crisp-tender; drain.

Melt butter in a saucepan; blend in flour and salt. Gradually stir in milk; cook over medium heat, stirring constantly, until sauce thickens. Add Worcestershire sauce, lemon juice, and onion juice. Just before serving, fold in chopped eggs.

Serve sauce over asparagus. Garnish with lemon, pimiento strips, and parsley. Yield: 6 to 8 servings.

Artichokes Stuffed with Crabmeat Louis

6 artichokes
1 teaspoon salt
1 teaspoon olive oil
1 pound crabmeat
Louis Sauce

Wash artichokes in cold water. Place enough water in a large saucepan to half cover the artichokes. Add salt and olive oil and bring to boil. Add artichokes; cover and simmer 25 to 30 minutes or until a leaf pulls out easily. Remove and drain. When cool, gently pull out center leaves, and scrape off the fuzzy thistle center (choke) with a spoon.

Combine crabmeat and about 1-1/2 cups Louis Sauce. Top artichokes with extra sauce. Yield: 6 servings.

Louis Sauce:

1 cup mayonnaise
1/4 cup whipping cream
1/4 teaspoon Worcestershire sauce
1/4 cup chopped green pepper
1/4 cup chopped green onion
2 tablespoons lemon juice

Combine ingredients in order given. Mix well and refrigerate 2 hours. Yield: 2 cups.

Strawberries Romanoff

2 quarts strawberries, halved
Sugar
1 pint vanilla ice cream, softened
1 cup whipping cream, whipped
Juice of 1 lemon
1/4 cup curaçao or other orange-flavored liqueur
2 tablespoons rum

Sweeten strawberries with sugar to taste; chill. When ready to serve, whip softened ice cream slightly and fold in whipped cream. Add remaining ingredients, stirring well. Spoon strawberries into chilled sherbet glasses, and top with whipped cream mixture. Yield: 10 to 12 servings.

Southern Strawberry Pie

3/4 cup sugar
2 tablespoons cornstarch
2 tablespoons light corn syrup
1 cup water
3 tablespoons strawberry-flavored gelatin
1 quart fresh strawberries
1 baked (9-inch) pastry shell

Combine sugar, cornstarch, corn syrup, and water in a saucepan; bring to a boil. Cook, stirring constantly, until clear and thickened. Add gelatin, stirring until dissolved. Cool.

Place strawberries in pastry shell; pour in gelatin mixture. Chill until firm. Yield: one 9-inch pie.

Asparagus Soup Marseilles

1 pound fresh asparagus spears
2-1/2 cups milk
1 teaspoon instant minced onion
1 teaspoon salt
1 teaspoon dry mustard
1/2 teaspoon capers
1/2 teaspoon juice from capers
Dash of pepper
Shredded lemon peel or chopped hard-cooked
    egg and pimiento strips

Cook asparagus; drain well, and chop. Combine asparagus, milk, and next 6 ingredients in container of electric blender; blend at high speed until smooth.

Pour asparagus soup into a saucepan; heat to serving temperature. Garnish with lemon peel. Yield: 4 cups.

Asparagus Vinaigrette

24 fresh asparagus spears, cooked and drained
1/2 cup vegetable oil
4 tablespoons wine vinegar
1/2 teaspoon salt
1/2 teaspoon dry mustard
1/2 teaspoon chopped onion
1 tablespoon chopped pimiento
Lettuce leaves
4 slices bacon, fried crisp and crumbled

Arrange asparagus spears in a dish. To make dressing, combine oil, vinegar, salt, mustard, onion, and pimiento; shake well, and pour half over asparagus. Cover. Marinate in refrigerator for 30 minutes.

Arrange asparagus spears on lettuce leaves. Shake remaining dressing well; pour over asparagus, and sprinkle with bacon. Yield: 6 servings.

Asparagus in Wine

2 pounds fresh asparagus spears
1/4 cup melted butter or margarine
1/4 cup white wine
1/2 teaspoon salt
1/4 teaspoon pepper
1/3 cup grated Parmesan cheese

Snap off tough ends of asparagus. Remove scales with knife or vegetable peeler.

Cook asparagus in boiling salted water about 10 minutes or until crisp tender; drain. Place in a greased, shallow 2-quart casserole dish. Combine butter and wine; pour over asparagus. Sprinkle with salt, pepper, and cheese. Bake at 425° for 15 minutes. Yield: 6 servings.

Marinated Asparagus

3 pounds fresh asparagus
About 1-1/2 cups oil-and-vinegar salad dressing

Break off tough end of each asparagus spear by bending stalk gently until it snaps easily. Wash spears thoroughly in warm water; drain well. Peel stalks with vegetable peeler to remove scales, or peel off tough scales with a knife.

Place asparagus in a shallow baking dish; pour salad dressing over spears. Cover tightly and chill 48 hours, turning asparagus occasionally. Drain well before serving. Yield: about 25 to 30 appetizer servings.

Symbolic bas relief from Musée Ochier, Cluny

Oriental Grilled Lamb Chops

8 to 12 (1-inch-thick) lamb chops
1/2 cup soy sauce
1/2 cup water
2 tablespoons sugar
1/2 teaspoon toasted sesame seeds
1/2 teaspoon fresh ground ginger
1 clove garlic, minced
Pepper to taste

Place meat in a shallow dish. Combine remaining ingredients; pour over meat. Cover and marinate in refrigerator 8 hours. Remove meat from the marinade.

Grill chops 5 to 6 inches from low to medium heat 30 to 35 minutes; turn several times. Yield: 4 to 6 servings.

Savory Lamb

1 (3-pound) boneless leg of lamb, cut into
    1-1/2-inch cubes
Salt and pepper to taste
1/4 cup olive oil
1-1/2 cups minced onion
2 cloves garlic, crushed
1/2 cup dry red wine
1 (6-ounce) can tomato paste
2 tablespoons wine vinegar
1 teaspoon ground thyme
Hot cooked rice

Place lamb in a mixing bowl, and sprinkle with salt and pepper; add oil, and stir to coat meat cubes. Place lamb, onion, and garlic in a Dutch oven.

Combine wine, tomato paste, vinegar, and thyme; blend well, and spoon over meat. Cover and bake at 325° for 1-1/2 to 2 hours, stirring occasionally. Serve over rice. Yield: 6 servings.

Wayne Thiebaud: **Sandwich**, *1963, Allan Stone Gallery, New York*

Open and Shut Case: The Sandwich

One useful function of British peers has been to lend their names to the language of everyday life. Lord Derby bestowed his name upon a horse race; Lord Brougham's became a buggy and a kind of automobile; Lord Raglan, having lost his arm in the Crimean War, invented the casual sleeve that bears his name; and Lord Cardigan, rising to greater heights, created the baggy sweater. But the most famous transformation of all came from John Montagu, fourth Earl of Sandwich. He was, legend tells us, such a dedicated gambler that he refused to leave the gaming tables even to eat. His solution was to have his servants bring him a piece of meat between two slices of bread, to be held in his left hand while he rolled the dice with his right. That was sometime before 1790, and it is hard to understand how the human race survived for so many years without a suitable word for a thing as portable, adaptable, nourishing, delicious, and generally serviceable as the sandwich. The *Sandwich* opposite was painted by Wayne Thiebaud, a modern realist painter who often depicts food. He has said that his aim is replication; he wants the food he paints to "look alive, fresh, and available," as indeed it does. But the reader is advised to turn the page anyway, for a taste of the real thing.

Hot Brown Sandwich photographed by Jerome Drown

Sandwiches

The sandwiches here range from hot and hearty to cool and crisp. For a light lunch or a quick supper, they offer imaginative alternatives to the predictable B.L.&T. or ham-and-swiss.

Hot Brown Sandwich

1/4 cup butter or margarine
1/2 cup all-purpose flour
1/2 teaspoon salt
1/8 teaspoon white pepper
1 cup turkey broth or chicken broth
1 cup milk
1/2 cup grated Parmesan cheese
8 slices bread, toasted
Sliced turkey
Paprika
8 slices tomato
8 slices bacon, cooked
Parsley

Melt butter, and stir in flour; cook over low heat, blending until smooth. Stir in salt and pepper. Gradually add broth and milk; cook, stirring constantly, until smooth and thickened. Add cheese; simmer about 10 minutes. (Sauce will be thick.)

Place 2 slices toast on each of 4 ovenproof plates. Place turkey on each slice of toast; cover with sauce, and sprinkle with paprika. Top each with 1 slice tomato and 1 slice bacon. Bake at 400° for 10 minutes or until sauce is bubbly. Garnish with parsley. Yield: 4 servings.

Drawing of a crab by Leonardo da Vinci. Kolnisches Stadtmuseum, Köln, Germany

Hot Topped Beefburgers

1 pound ground beef
1 teaspoon salt
Dash of pepper
1 tablespoon Worcestershire sauce
1 tablespoon grated onion
1/4 cup cold water
Blue cheese topping (recipe follows)
Mustard topping (recipe follows)
4 hamburger buns, split

Combine beef, salt, pepper, Worcestershire sauce, onion, and water; mix thoroughly. Shape into 8 thin patties. Broil 2 to 4 minutes on each side, depending on desired degree of doneness.

Spread an equal amount of blue cheese topping or mustard topping on each patty; broil until topping is hot and bubbly. Place a patty on each bun half. Yield: 8 open-faced sandwiches.

Blue Cheese Topping:
1/2 cup butter or margarine, softened
2 tablespoons crumbled blue cheese
Combine butter and blue cheese, mixing until smooth. Yield: about 1/2 cup.

Mustard Topping:
1/4 cup butter or margarine, softened
1-1/2 tablespoons dry mustard
Combine butter and dry mustard, mixing until smooth. Yield: about 1/4 cup.

Creamy Crab Sandwich

1 (8-ounce) package cream cheese, softened
1/4 teaspoon butter or margarine
1 teaspoon Worcestershire sauce
1 tablespoon chopped onion
1 teaspoon prepared mustard
1 tablespoon lemon juice
1 (6-ounce) package frozen crabmeat, thawed and drained
4 English muffins, split
4 tomato slices
4 slices process American cheese
8 slices bacon, cooked and halved

Combine first 6 ingredients; beat until fluffy. Fold in crabmeat. Spread mixture on English muffins. Top each with a tomato slice, a cheese slice, and two pieces bacon. Bake at 350° for 8 to 10 minutes. Yield: 8 servings.

Mushrooms Magnifique

1 medium onion, chopped
1 pound fresh mushrooms, thinly sliced
2 tablespoons butter or margarine
Salt and pepper to taste
Chopped parsley
Paprika
1 tablespoon lemon juice
1-1/2 cups commercial sour cream
6 slices Canadian bacon
3 English muffins, halved and toasted

Sauté onion and mushrooms in butter until tender. Add salt, pepper, parsley, paprika, lemon juice, and sour cream; place over low heat until warm. (Do not allow to boil.)

Fry Canadian bacon, and place on muffin halves. Spoon sauce over bacon. Serve immediately. Yield: 6 servings.

Baked Hero Sandwiches

1-1/2 pounds ground chuck
1 (6-ounce) can tomato paste
1-1/2 tablespoons catsup
1 tablespoon finely chopped onion
1/4 cup finely chopped mushrooms
1/4 teaspoon garlic salt
1/4 teaspoon pepper
1 tablespoon sloppy Joe seasoning mix or spaghetti sauce mix
6 hero rolls, split
Melted butter
6 slices American, Cheddar, or mozzarella cheese
12 green pepper rings
12 thin slices tomato

Combine meat, tomato paste, catsup, onion, mushrooms, garlic salt, pepper, and seasoning mix in a large bowl; mix thoroughly.

Brush rolls with butter, and place on an ungreased baking sheet. Spoon about 2 tablespoons meat mixture on each half of roll, spreading evenly to edges of rolls. Bake sandwiches at 425° for 20 to 25 minutes. Turn off oven and remove sandwiches.

Cut cheese slices in half diagonally; place one piece on each sandwich. Return to oven to melt cheese. Garnish with green pepper rings and tomato slices. Yield: 12 servings.

Note: Meat mixture may be prepared ahead and refrigerated or frozen until needed.

Corny Sandwich Squares

1 (8-ounce) package cornbread mix
1 (8-3/4-ounce) can cream-style corn
2 eggs
2 tablespoons milk
1-1/4 cups shredded American cheese, divided
1 pound ground beef
1/4 cup catsup
2 tablespoons sweet pickle relish
1/4 cup grated Parmesan cheese
1/4 cup water
1 tablespoon cornstarch
1 (16-ounce) can stewed tomatoes, diced
1 teaspoon Worcestershire sauce

Combine cornbread mix, corn, eggs, milk, and 3/4 cup American cheese; stir until blended. Spread half of batter in a greased 8-inch square baking dish; set aside.

Brown ground beef. Drain; add catsup and relish. Spread mixture over batter; sprinkle with remaining 1/2 cup American cheese and Parmesan cheese. Top with remaining batter. Bake at 350° for 35 minutes.

Combine water and cornstarch in a saucepan; stir in tomatoes and Worcestershire sauce. Cook over medium heat, stirring constantly, until thick. Let sandwiches stand 5 minutes before cutting into squares; serve topped with sauce. Yield: about 6 servings.

Devonshire Sandwiches

18 slices bacon
1/2 cup all-purpose flour
2 cups milk
1/2 pound Cheddar cheese, shredded
1 teaspoon dry mustard
6 slices bread
12 thin slices chicken or turkey breast
1/4 cup grated Parmesan cheese

Cook bacon; drain, reserving 1/4 cup drippings. Combine flour and reserved drippings over low heat, blending until smooth. Gradually add milk; cook until smooth and thickened, stirring constantly. Add Cheddar cheese and dry mustard, stirring until cheese melts.

Place 3 slices bacon on each slice of bread, and top with 2 slices of chicken. Place in a 13- x 9-1/2- x 2-inch baking pan; cover with cheese sauce, and sprinkle with Parmesan cheese. Bake at 350° for 10 minutes or until bubbly. Yield: 6 sandwiches.

Celebration Sandwich Loaf

1 (16-inch) loaf white bread, unsliced
Butter or margarine, softened
Fillings (recipes follow)
3 (8-ounce) packages cream cheese, softened
1/2 cup mayonnaise
Minced parsley

Trim crust from sides and top of bread. Slice loaf horizontally into 5 equal slices. Place bottom slice on serving platter or tray. Spread with butter; cover with one of the fillings.

Spread remaining slices on both sides with butter. Place one buttered slice of bread on top of filling and bread on tray; cover with another filling. Repeat layers until all fillings are used and loaf is reassembled. Chill.

Beat cream cheese and mayonnaise until smooth. Frost top and sides of loaf with cream cheese mixture. Chill. Garnish with parsley before serving. Yield: about 12 servings.

Ham Filling:
1-1/2 cups ground cooked ham
1/3 cup pickle relish
1 tablespoon prepared mustard
1/2 cup mayonnaise

Combine all ingredients. Chill. Yield: about 2-1/2 cups.

Tuna Filling:
1 (6-1/2-ounce) can tuna, drained and flaked
1/3 cup sliced ripe olives
Salt and pepper
1/4 cup mayonnaise

Combine all ingredients. Chill. Yield: about 2 cups.

Egg Filling:
6 hard-cooked eggs, chopped
1 tablespoon chives
2 tablespoons chopped pimiento
Salt and pepper
1/4 cup mayonnaise

Combine all ingredients. Chill. Yield: about 2 cups.

Chicken Filling:
1-1/2 cups ground cooked chicken
2/3 cup crushed pineapple, well drained
1/4 cup chopped green pepper
1/3 cup mayonnaise

Combine all ingredients. Chill. Yield: about 2-1/2 cups.

Golden Sandwich Puffs

6 slices white bread, toasted
Butter or margarine
2 medium tomatoes, sliced
6 slices sharp process American cheese
1 pound fresh asparagus spears, cooked and drained
3 eggs, separated
Dash of salt
Dash of pepper
1 tablespoon French dressing

Spread toast with butter; place buttered side up on baking sheet. Top with tomato slices, cheese slices, and asparagus spears.

Beat egg yolks until thick and lemon colored; add salt, pepper, and French dressing. Beat egg whites until stiff peaks form. Fold egg yolk mixture into egg whites; spoon over asparagus.

Bake at 350° about 15 minutes or until egg mixture is lightly browned. Yield: 6 servings.

Reuben Sandwiches

16 slices rye or pumpernickel bread
1/4 to 1/2 cup butter or margarine, softened
About 3/4 cup Thousand Island dressing
8 slices corned beef
8 slices Swiss cheese
About 2-1/2 cups sauerkraut, well drained

Spread one side of each slice of bread with butter. Place 8 slices of bread, buttered side down, on a lightly greased griddle or skillet; spread Thousand Island dressing on top side. Top each slice with corned beef, cheese, and sauerkraut.

Spread Thousand Island dressing on unbuttered side of remaining bread slices. Place these, dressing side down, on top of sandwiches. Grill slowly until cheese melts and bread browns; turn and grill other side. Yield: 8 servings.

Dagwood, America's supreme sandwich chef.
© *King Features Syndicate, Inc.* 1978

119

Mary Cassatt: A Cup of Tea, *c. 1880, Museum of Fine Arts, Boston*

Coffee, Tea, and Ceremony

From a chemist's point of view, tea and coffee are merely hot water with flavoring: they contain no protein, no vitamins—nothing in any way nourishing. But nutrition is not everything in life. People enjoy imbibing flavored hot water at regular intervals and find their deepest needs satisfied by the drink as much as by meat and potatoes. Coffee and tea provide us, among other things, with a reason to sit down in midafternoon with friends and a slice of something good. The painting opposite, of two tea drinkers beside a silver tea service in a cozy Victorian drawing room, was made in 1880 by Mary Cassatt, the American Impressionist painter. In the late nineteenth century, an afternoon tea like this one was a genuine social occasion. The list of foods customarily set on the tea table in a fine home was daunting: toast and jam, biscuits, scones, pâtés, chicken and lobster salads, sandwiches of every description, pastries, three or four kinds of cake. Compared with such a spread, the coffee ring at right and the other foods whose recipes follow are of a modest scale. They are rich enough, however, to sustain a kindly custom: an hour of civilized conversation around the tea- or coffeepot in the middle of the afternoon.

Filled Coffee Ring photographed by Jerome Drown

Coffee Break

It was just after the Civil War that coffee emerged as America's national drink. Since then, the coffee break has become a national reflex, written into union contracts and heralded aloft in the "Coffee, tea, or milk" chant of the airline stewardess. Accompanied by muffins, coffee cake, or fruit bread, the straightforward tea or coffee break is happily elaborated into a ceremony.

Speedy Danish Coffee Cake

1 package dry yeast
1/4 cup warm water (105° to 115°)
2 cups all-purpose flour
4 tablespoons sugar, divided
1 teaspoon salt
1 cup butter or margarine
1 egg, beaten
1 teaspoon vanilla extract
Fruit Filling

Dissolve yeast in warm water; set aside. Combine flour, 2 tablespoons sugar, and salt; cut in butter with a pastry blender. Combine yeast mixture, egg, and vanilla; stir into flour mixture, blending until smooth.

Place dough on a floured surface, and roll into a 14- x 10-inch rectangle. Place in a greased 11- x 7- x 2-inch pan; allow extra dough to hang over sides of pan. Spread Fruit Filling over dough, and fold overhanging dough over fruit.

Sprinkle dough with remaining 2 tablespoons sugar. Bake at 375° for 30 minutes; reduce heat to 300°, and bake 15 to 20 minutes or until lightly browned. Yield: about 6 servings.

Fruit Filling:
2/3 cup cooked, chopped prunes
2/3 cup cooked, chopped apricots
1 (8-ounce) can crushed pineapple, undrained
1/2 cup sugar
1-1/2 tablespoons quick-cooking tapioca

Combine all ingredients, mixing well. Yield: about 2-1/3 cups.

Eggnog Doughnuts

1 cup eggnog
1/4 cup butter or margarine
1/3 cup sugar
1/2 teaspoon salt
3-1/3 cups all-purpose flour, divided
2 packages dry yeast
3/4 teaspoon ground nutmeg
2 eggs
Vegetable oil
Eggnog Glaze

Combine eggnog, butter, sugar, and salt in a small saucepan; place over low heat until butter melts, stirring constantly. Set aside, and let cool to 105° to 115°.

Combine 2 cups flour, yeast, and nutmeg; add warm eggnog mixture, and mix well. Add eggs, and beat at low speed of electric mixer 30 seconds, scraping bowl constantly; beat at high speed 3 minutes longer. Stir in remaining 1-1/3 cups flour by hand, mixing well. Place dough in a greased bowl, turning once to grease top. Cover and chill at least 2 to 3 hours.

Punch dough down, and turn out on a lightly floured surface. Cover and let rest 10 minutes. Roll to 1/3-inch thickness, and cut with a floured doughnut cutter. Place doughnuts several inches apart on a greased baking sheet; cover and let rise in a warm place until very light (about 45 to 50 minutes).

Place doughnuts, a few at a time, in deep oil heated to 375°; fry until golden brown on both sides (about 1-1/2 to 2 minutes), turning once. Drain well on paper towels. While still warm, dip top of each in Eggnog Glaze. Yield: about 2 dozen.

Eggnog Glaze:
2 cups sifted powdered sugar
3 tablespoons eggnog
Dash of ground nutmeg

Combine all ingredients, and mix until smooth. Yield: about 1-1/2 cups.

Coffee-house tokens.
Courtesy of Guildhall Library, London

Sopaipilla

1-3/4 cups all-purpose flour
2 teaspoons baking powder
1 tablespoon sugar
1 teaspoon salt
2 tablespoons shortening
2/3 cup milk
2 cups hot vegetable oil
Honey
Cinnamon sugar

Combine flour, baking powder, sugar, and salt in a large mixing bowl. Cut in shortening with pastry blender or fork until mixture resembles cornmeal. Add milk, mixing just until dough holds together in a ball.

Turn out onto a lightly floured surface; knead gently, about 1 minute, until smooth. Cover dough, and let rest for 1 hour.

Roll into a 12- x 15-inch rectangle with a floured rolling pin; dough should be 1/16 to 1/8 inch thick. Cut into 3-inch squares or 2- x 3-inch oblongs.

Heat oil in a saucepan to 370° to 380°. Drop a few pieces of dough at a time into the oil, turning at once so they will puff evenly. Turn back over, and brown both sides. Drain on absorbent paper towels.

Serve hot with honey and cinnamon sugar. Yield about 20 servings.

Fresh Apple Coffee Cake

1 cup sugar
1/2 cup shortening
1 egg
1-1/2 cups all-purpose flour
1 teaspoon soda
1 teaspoon salt
2 cups peeled, chopped apple
2 tablespoons all-purpose flour
1/3 cup firmly packed brown sugar
1 teaspoon ground cinnamon
1/2 cup chopped pecans

Cream sugar and shortening until light and fluffy; add egg, and beat well. Combine 1-1/2 cups flour, soda, and salt; add to creamed mixture, mixing well.

Combine apple with 2 tablespoons flour; stir into batter. Pour batter into a greased 10- x 6- x 2-inch baking dish. Combine brown sugar, cinnamon, and pecans; sprinkle over batter. Bake at 350° for 40 minutes. Yield: 8 servings.

Filled Coffee Ring

2 packages dry yeast
1/2 cup warm water (105° to 115°)
1-1/2 cups lukewarm milk
1 cup sugar, divided
2 teaspoons salt
2 eggs, beaten
1/2 cup vegetable oil
6-1/2 to 7-1/2 cups all-purpose flour
1/4 cup melted butter or margarine
2 tablespoons ground cinnamon
3 tablespoons raisins
3 tablespoons chopped maraschino cherries
3 tablespoons chopped pecans
Creamy Frosting

Dissolve yeast in warm water; set aside 5 minutes. Combine milk, 1/2 cup sugar, and salt; stir in yeast mixture, eggs, and oil. Add enough flour to make a soft but slightly sticky dough; mix well. Cover and let rise in a warm place, free from drafts, until doubled in bulk (about 1 hour).

Turn dough out on a floured surface, and knead until smooth and elastic (about 5 minutes). Return dough to bowl; cover and again let rise until doubled (about 40 minutes).

Place dough on a floured surface, and roll into a 21- x 12-inch rectangle. Spread with melted butter; sprinkle with remaining 1/2 cup sugar, cinnamon, raisins, cherries, and pecans. Starting at long edge, roll dough up jellyroll fashion; pinch edges together to seal.

Place roll on a greased cookie sheet; shape into a ring, and pinch ends together to seal. Using kitchen shears or a sharp knife, make a cut every inch around ring (cut should go two-thirds of way through roll).

Gently pull slices out and twist, overlapping slightly. Cover and let rise in a warm place, free from drafts, until doubled in bulk (about 30 minutes).

Bake at 350° for 20 to 25 minutes or until done. Drizzle Creamy Frosting over hot ring. Yield: 16 to 20 servings.

Creamy Frosting:
1 cup whipping cream
1 cup sugar
1 teaspoon almond or vanilla extract

Combine all ingredients in a saucepan. Cook, stirring constantly, over low heat until mixture reaches soft ball stage (230°). Remove from heat, and beat until thickened. Yield: about 1-1/4 cups.

Cranberry Coffee Cake

1/2 cup butter or margarine, softened
1 cup sugar
2 eggs
2 cups all-purpose flour
1 teaspoon baking powder
1 teaspoon soda
1/2 teaspoon salt
1 (8-ounce) carton commercial sour cream
1 teaspoon almond extract
1 (16-ounce) can whole-berry cranberry sauce
1/2 cup chopped pecans
Glaze (optional)

Cream butter and sugar until light and fluffy. Add eggs, one at a time, beating thoroughly after each addition. Combine flour, baking powder, soda, and salt; add to creamed mixture alternately with sour cream, beating well after each addition. Add flavoring, and mix well.

Spoon one-third of mixture into a greased and floured 10-inch tube pan. Spread one-third of cranberry sauce over batter. Repeat layers twice more, ending with cranberry sauce. Sprinkle pecans over top.

Bake at 350° for 1 hour or until cake tests done. Let cool 5 minutes before removing from pan. Drizzle glaze over top, if desired. Yield: one 10-inch cake.

Glaze:
3/4 cup powdered sugar
1/2 teaspoon almond extract
1 tablespoon warm water

Combine all ingredients; stir well.

Blueberry Gems

2 cups self-rising flour
1-1/2 cups sugar
2 eggs, slightly beaten
1 teaspoon vanilla extract
1/2 cup vegetable oil
1/2 cup milk
1 cup blueberries

Combine flour and sugar in a large bowl; set aside. Combine eggs, vanilla, oil, and milk. Make a well in the center of dry ingredients; pour in liquid ingredients. Stir until well mixed. Fold in blueberries; stir 1 minute.

Spoon batter into muffin tins, filling about half full. Bake at 375° for 25 minutes. Yield: about 2 dozen muffins.

Christmas Stollen

1 cup milk
1 cup melted butter or margarine
1/2 cup water
5-1/4 cups all-purpose flour
1/4 cup sugar
1 teaspoon salt
2 packages dry yeast
2 eggs, beaten
1/2 teaspoon grated lemon rind
1/2 teaspoon grated orange rind
1/2 cup seedless raisins
1/2 cup chopped candied fruit
1/2 cup chopped nuts
3 tablespoons butter or margarine, softened
1/2 cup sugar
1 tablespoon ground cinnamon
1 cup powdered sugar
2 to 3 tablespoons water or milk
1/4 teaspoon vanilla extract
Candied cherry halves

Combine milk, 1 cup melted butter, and 1/2 cup water in a small saucepan; place over low heat just until lukewarm.

Combine flour, 1/4 cup sugar, salt, and yeast in a large mixing bowl; stir in warm milk mixture and eggs, mixing well. Add lemon and orange rind, raisins, fruit, and nuts; mix well. Cover dough, and refrigerate overnight.

Place chilled dough on a floured surface; roll into an 18- x 12-inch rectangle; spread with 3 tablespoons soft butter. Combine 1/2 cup sugar and cinnamon; sprinkle over butter.

Beginning with long edge, roll up dough jellyroll fashion, pinching edges to seal; if ends are smaller than remainder of roll, trim off about 1 inch. Place roll on a large greased cookie sheet, and shape into a ring (it should resemble a large doughnut). Brush ends of roll with water, and pinch together to seal.

Using kitchen shears, make cuts in dough every inch around ring, cutting two-thirds of the way through roll at each cut. Gently turn each piece of dough on its side, slightly overlapping the previous piece.

Let rise in a warm place, uncovered, 1 hour. Bake at 350° for 25 to 30 minutes or until golden brown.

Combine powdered sugar, 2 tablespoons water, and vanilla; drizzle over hot ring. Decorate with candied cherry halves. Yield: 12 to 16 servings.

W. Bennett after A. C. Pugin: **The Great Kitchen, Royal Pavilion, Brighton,** *1818-25, Cooper-Hewitt Museum, New York*

O For Friends and Family

One of the several great stars of classic French cuisine was Marie-Antoine Carême. Born in poverty in Paris in 1784, he began his career making rabbit fricassee in a local eating house. He ended up a wealthy man, chef to George IV of England. Opposite is a view of Carême's kitchen at the Brighton Pavilion, the seaside playhouse of the King. At least a dozen cooks are hard at work, and the central table is crowded with silver serving dishes, for a typical royal dinner, as orchestrated by Carême, might begin with four kinds of soup, followed by four kinds of fish, each in a different sauce, and then ham, goose, chicken, and veal. These main dishes would be set on the table with more than thirty subsidiary entrées, all of which constituted merely the first course. Afterward came game and roasts and a variety of vegetables, succeeded, in turn, by a parade of elaborate desserts. Not every guest was expected to sample every dish—the logistics would have been impossible. Yet even the King once complained that Carême was feeding him too well. "You will make me die of indigestion," he is reported to have told Carême, and the chef replied, "I am supposed to flatter your appetite, not regulate it." Gourmandism in the grand style has, mercifully, gone out of fashion, but there are still special occasions that call for a table more bounteously laid than usual. One of them, of course, is Thanksgiving. To prepare the feast at right would not require the labor of twelve chefs or a half-acre kitchen. And while Carême and his mentor might think it modest, modern celebrants will find it a meal fit for any king.

The recipes for this dinner,
photographed by Jerome Drown, follow.

Dinner

Good guests at a good dinner present one of the few possibilities for human perfection — the first willing to accept almost anything, the second willing to give almost everything.

Oyster Stew

1 quart half-and-half or milk
2 tablespoons butter or margarine
2 green onions, chopped
1 pint oysters, undrained
Salt to taste
Red pepper to taste

Heat half-and-half in top of a double boiler until hot but not boiling. Melt butter in a saucepan over medium heat; add onion, and sauté lightly. Add oysters, and cook until edges begin to curl. Combine oyster mixture with half-and-half; stir in salt and red pepper. Serve with crackers. Yield: 6 to 8 servings.

Baked Country Ham

1 (15-pound) sugar-cured country ham
About 1 (16-ounce) package light brown sugar
Whole cloves

Scrub ham thoroughly with a stiff brush; do not soak. Pour water to 1-1/2-inch depth in a large roasting pan. Place ham, skin side down, in roaster; coat exposed portion generously with brown sugar. Cover and bake at 350° for 4 hours, basting with pan juices every 20 to 30 minutes.

Carefully remove ham from water; remove skin. Place ham, fat side up, on a cutting board; score fat in a diamond design, and stud with cloves.

Return ham to roaster, fat side up; coat top generously with brown sugar. Continue baking, uncovered, for 1 hour. Yield: about 30 servings.

Note: A larger or smaller ham may be substituted. Bake 20 minutes per pound; uncover during last hour of baking time, after fat is scored and studded with cloves.

Old-Fashioned Roast Turkey

Select a 12- to 14-pound turkey. Remove giblets, and rinse turkey thoroughly with cold water; pat dry. Sprinkle inside cavity with salt. Tie ends of legs to tail with cord or string, or tuck them under flap of skin around tail. Lift wingtips up and over back so they are tucked under bird.

Brush entire bird with melted butter or margarine; place on a roasting rack, breast side up. Insert meat thermometer in breast or meaty part of thigh, making sure it does not touch bone. Bake at 325° until meat thermometer reaches 185° (about 4-1/2 to 5 hours). If turkey starts to get too brown, cover lightly with aluminum foil.

When turkey is two-thirds done, cut the cord or band of skin holding the drumstick ends to the tail; this will ensure that the inside of the thighs is cooked. Turkey is done when drumsticks are easy to move up and down. Garnish with spiced crabapples and parsley. Yield: 20 to 24 servings.

"Southern" Giblet Gravy

Giblets from 1 turkey
Turkey neck
2 cups chicken broth
1 medium onion, chopped
1 cup chopped celery
1/2 teaspoon poultry seasoning
1/2 cup cornbread dressing
Salt and pepper to taste
2 hard-cooked eggs, sliced

Cook giblets and turkey neck in chicken broth until tender (about 2 hours). Remove meat from broth, discard neck, chop giblets, return to broth.

Add onion, celery, poultry seasoning, and dressing to broth mixture; cook until vegetables are tender. Stir in salt, pepper, and egg slices. If thicker gravy is desired, add dressing. Yield: about 2 cups.

Note: Flour may be used instead of dressing to thicken gravy. Dissolve 2 tablespoons flour in a small amount of water, and stir into broth.

Parslied New Potatoes

3 pounds small new potatoes, scraped
5 cups water
Salt to taste
3/4 cup melted butter or margarine
6 tablespoons minced parsley

Cook potatoes in boiling salted water until tender; drain well. Combine butter and parsley; spoon over hot potatoes. Yield: 8 servings.

Detail of Perry's Preparing for Thanksgiving Dinner, *courtesy Addison Gallery*

Southwest Cornbread Dressing

2 (6-ounce) packages cornbread mix
1 cup chopped celery
1 cup chopped green onion
1/2 cup chopped green pepper
1 clove garlic, minced
1/2 cup melted butter or margarine
Turkey giblets
2 slices bread
1 (10-3/4-ounce) can chicken broth
3 eggs, slightly beaten
6 tamales, mashed
1/2 teaspoon salt
Crushed red pepper to taste

Prepare cornbread mix according to package directions; cool. Crumble cornbread into a large bowl, and set aside. Sauté celery, onion, green pepper, and garlic in butter until soft. Stir into cornbread, and set aside.

Put giblets in a saucepan; cover with water, and bring to a boil. Reduce heat; cover and simmer until tender. Chop liver; add to cornbread mixture along with 1/3 cup stock. Reserve remaining giblets for gravy.

Soak bread in chicken broth, and stir into cornbread mixture. Add remaining ingredients, mixing thoroughly. Spoon into a greased 2-quart casserole. Bake at 350° for 30 to 35 minutes. Yield: about 8 servings.

Green Bean Casserole

2 (16-ounce) cans French-cut green beans,
    drained
2 (10-3/4-ounce) cans cream of mushroom soup,
    undiluted
1 cup diced celery
1 cup diced green pepper
1 cup diced onion
5 to 6 ripe olives, sliced
3/4 cup crushed potato chips
1/4 cup slivered almonds
5 to 6 pimiento-stuffed olives, sliced

Layer half of beans, soup, celery, green pepper,
and onion in a buttered 2-quart casserole; repeat
layers. Top with a layer of ripe olives, potato chips,
almonds, and stuffed olives. Bake at 325° for 35 to
40 minutes. Yield: about 8 servings.

Apricot Dream Salad

2 (6-ounce) packages dried apricots
3/4 cup water
1/2 cup sugar
3 (3-ounce) packages lemon-flavored gelatin
5 cups boiling water
1 (20-ounce) can crushed pineapple, drained
1 cup slivered almonds
Deluxe Dressing

Combine apricots and 3/4 cup water in a saucepan; simmer until tender. Remove from heat, and
stir in sugar. Mash with a fork until smooth, and
set aside 1/2 cup for dressing.

Dissolve gelatin in boiling water. Stir in remaining apricot mixture, pineapple, and almonds. Pour
into a 13- x 9- x 2-inch pan or individual molds.
Chill until firm. Cut into squares, and top with
Deluxe Dressing before serving. Yield: about 15
servings.

Deluxe Dressing:
1 (8-ounce) package cream cheese, softened
1/2 cup reserved mashed apricots
2 tablespoons sherry
1/2 pint whipping cream, divided
1/4 cup powdered sugar
1/2 teaspoon vanilla extract
1/2 teaspoon almond extract

Combine cream cheese, apricots, sherry, and 4
tablespoons cream; beat until smooth. Whip remaining cream; add powdered sugar and flavorings.
Fold into cream cheese mixture. Yield: about 2-1/2
cups.

Cran-Apple Relish

1 orange, unpeeled
5 to 6 red apples, unpeeled
1 (1-pound) bag fresh cranberries, washed
2 cups sugar
1 (20-ounce) can crushed pineapple, well drained
1/2 cup chopped pecans

Quarter and seed orange and apples. Coarsely
grind cranberries, orange, and apples in a food
grinder or blender. Add sugar, pineapple, and
pecans; mix well. Refrigerate overnight. Yield: 2
quarts.

Charlotte Russe

4 eggs, separated
10 tablespoons sugar, divided
1 envelope unflavored gelatin
1/2 cup cold water
1 pint whipping cream, whipped
1 teaspoon vanilla extract
12 to 18 ladyfingers

Beat egg yolks and 4 tablespoons sugar until
thick and lemon colored; set aside. Soften gelatin
in cold water; place over hot water and stir until
dissolved. Add gelatin to yolk mixture.

Beat egg whites in a large bowl; gradually add 6
tablespoons sugar and continue to beat until stiff
peaks form. Reserve 1/2 cup whipped cream for
garnish. Fold remaining whipped cream, yolk
mixture, and vanilla into egg whites.

Split ladyfingers in half lengthwise. Line an 8-
cup glass or crystal bowl with ladyfingers. Pour in
filling; chill until set. Garnish with reserved 1/2
cup whipped cream. Yield: 8 to 10 servings.

Note: Individual compotes may be used. Quarter
ladyfingers lengthwise. Line compotes, and fill
as directed.

*Angels making ice cream depicted in an old
print from the New York Public Library*

Light Fruitcake

1-1/2 cups butter, softened
1-1/2 cups sugar
1 tablespoon vanilla extract
1 tablespoon lemon extract
7 eggs, separated and at room temperature
3 cups all-purpose flour
1-1/2 pounds candied yellow, green, and red
    pineapple (about 3 cups)
1 pound candied red and green cherries
    (about 2 cups)
1/4 pound candied citron (about 1/2 cup)
1/2 pound golden raisins (about 1-1/2 cups)
3 cups pecan halves
1 cup black walnuts, coarsely chopped
1/2 cup all-purpose flour
Additional candied fruit and nuts (optional)
1/4 cup brandy
Additional brandy

Make a liner for a 10-inch tube pan by drawing
a circle with an 18-inch diameter on a piece of
brown paper. Cut out circle; set pan in center, and
draw around base of pan and inside tube. Fold
circle into eighths, having the drawn lines on the
outside.

Cut off tip end of circle along inside drawn line.
Unfold paper; cut along folds to the outside drawn
line. From another piece of brown paper, cut another circle with a 10-inch diameter; grease and
set aside. Place the 18-inch liner in pan; grease
and set aside.

Cream butter and sugar until light and fluffy.
Stir in flavorings. Beat egg yolks. Alternately add
egg yolks and 3 cups flour to creamed mixture.

Combine candied fruit, raisins, and nuts in a
large mixing bowl; dredge with 1/2 cup flour,
stirring to coat well. Stir mixture into batter. Beat
egg whites until stiff; then fold into batter.

Spoon batter into prepared pan. Arrange additional fruit and nuts on top, if desired. Cover pan
with greased 10-inch brown paper circle. Bake at
250° for 2-1/2 to 3 hours or until cake tests done.
Remove from oven. Take off paper cover, and
slowly pour 1/4 cup brandy evenly over cake; cool
on rack.

Remove cake from pan; peel paper liner from
cake. Wrap cake in brandy-soaked cheesecloth
or clothlike disposable wiper. Store in an airtight
container in a cool place 3 weeks. Pour a small
amount of brandy over cake each week. Yield:
one 10-inch cake.

Note: Cake may be baked in 4 (9- x 5- x 3-inch)
paper-lined loafpans. Bake at 250° for 1-1/2 hours
or until done.

Anonymous Tavern Sign, 1800's, Connecticut Historical Society, Hartford

Regional Pleasures

Dining out is one of the great pleasures of traveling these days — if not its main purpose — but when travelers had to go by stagecoach or horseback over hazardous dirt roads that turned to knee-deep mud in the rain, there was no telling what might be waiting at the end of a long day's journey. With a bit of advance planning, the wayfarer might wind up at a "Strangers Resort," as advertised on the signboard opposite by an early Connecticut innkeeper named J. Carter — no relation to the Georgia branch, as far as anyone knows. Inns and taverns were very often run by women; hotelkeeping was one of a number of respectable occupations that Colonial females might follow. Old newspapers are full of their notices. One Mary Davis set up shop in Williamsburg in the mid-eighteenth century offering "12 or 14 very good lodging rooms, with fireplaces to most of them, which will hold two or three beds each." At another Virginia lodging house, the hostess offered a comforting variety of rums, beers, "cyders," clarets, ales, and a choice of "warm or cold diet." A bed to oneself cost sixpence, with a downward scale for double or triple occupancy — of the bed, not the room. Clean sheets, of course, cost extra. The quality of the victuals depended on any number of imponderables: the skill of the cook, the time of day and the season of the year, and local custom. But though the risks of dyspepsia were quite real, travelers must surely have enjoyed unique regional specialties. Such a feast of appealing oddments is set out at the right — roast turkey with peanut dressing, giblet gravy, fresh cranberry sauce, green beans, scalloped potatoes, yeast bread, corn relish, pie, and apple juice shrub.

Dinner at Wayside Inn (see recipes) photographed by Charles Beck

Regional

There was a time when the discerning traveler in the South could tell where he was by the style and substance of the food he ate. While the following dinner comes from one particular inn, the recipes tell us what can still be found, and once was to be had, by the traveler whose expectations did not dim with distance.

Old-Fashioned Yeast Bread

2 packages dry yeast
1/2 cup warm water (105° to 115°)
1 egg, well beaten
1 cup milk
1/4 cup sugar
2 tablespoons butter or margarine
1 tablespoon salt
5 to 6 cups sifted all-purpose flour
Melted butter or margarine

Dissolve yeast in warm water in a large mixing bowl; add egg, stirring well. Let stand 10 minutes.

Combine milk, sugar, butter, and salt in a small saucepan. Scald milk mixture, and cool to luke-warm; add to yeast mixture. Gradually stir in enough flour to make a soft dough that leaves sides of bowl.

Turn dough out on a lightly floured surface, and knead 5 minutes or until smooth and elastic. Shape into a ball; place in a greased bowl, turning to grease top. Cover and let rise in a warm place (85°), free from drafts, 1-1/2 hours or until doubled in bulk.

Punch dough down, and knead 1 minute. Shape into a ball, and place in greased bowl; cover and let rise 1 hour or until doubled in bulk.

Punch dough down again and divide into 3 equal portions. Shape each portion into a 6- x 3-inch loaf. Place loaves into 3 greased 7- x 3-1/2- x 2-inch loaf-pans. Cover and let rise 1 hour or until doubled in bulk. Bake at 325° for 20 minutes or until loaf sounds hollow when tapped. Remove from pans; brush with melted butter, and cool on wire racks. Yield: 3 loaves.

Roast Turkey with Peanut Dressing

1 (12- to 14-pound) turkey
Salt
Peanut Dressing
Melted butter, margarine, or vegetable oil

Remove giblets from large cavity; remove neck from neck cavity. Rinse turkey thoroughly with cold water and pat dry. Rub the cavities lightly with salt. Fill neck cavity with a small amount of Peanut Dressing and fasten skin to back with a skewer; lightly stuff large cavity. Fold the bird's wingtips across the back; tuck drumsticks under band of skin at tail, or tie them to the tail.

Brush entire bird with melted butter; place on a roasting rack, breast side up. Insert meat thermometer in thickest part of thigh, making sure it does not touch bone. Bake at 325° until meat thermometer reaches 185° (about 4-1/2 to 5 hours).

If turkey starts to brown too much, cover loosely with a tent of aluminum foil. When turkey is two-thirds done, cut band of skin or string holding drumsticks. Turkey is done when drumsticks are easy to move up and down.

Let turkey stand 15 to 20 minutes before carving. Yield: 14 to 16 servings.

Peanut Dressing:
3/4 cup finely chopped onion
1-1/2 cups finely chopped celery
1/2 cup chopped fresh parsley
1 cup melted margarine
12 cups soft breadcrumbs
2 cups salted peanuts, chopped
1 tablespoon salt
1 teaspoon pepper
1 tablespoon rubbed sage
4-1/2 cups water

Sauté onion, celery, and parsley in margarine in a large Dutch oven until tender. Add remaining ingredients; mix well and spoon into turkey cavities. Spoon remaining dressing into a greased baking dish; bake at 350° for 45 minutes to 1 hour or until lightly browned around edges. Yield: about 12 servings.

Wayside Scalloped Potatoes

8 large potatoes, peeled and sliced
1 large onion, sliced
1/4 cup butter or margarine
1/2 cup all-purpose flour
1/2 teaspoon dry mustard
2 cups milk
1 teaspoon Worcestershire sauce
1 pound sharp Cheddar cheese, shredded
1/4 cup breadcrumbs
Paprika

Cook potatoes and onion in a small amount of boiling salted water about 10 to 12 minutes, or until tender; drain well.

Melt butter in a large, heavy saucepan over low heat; add flour and mustard, stirring until smooth. Cook 1 minute, stirring constantly. Gradually add milk; cook over medium heat, stirring constantly, until thickened and bubbly. Add Worcestershire sauce and cheese, stirring until cheese melts.

Alternate layers of potato-onion mixture and cheese sauce in lightly greased, shallow 2-quart casserole. Top with breadcrumbs and sprinkle with paprika. Bake at 350° for 30 minutes or until bubbly. Yield: 10 servings.

Southern-Style Green Beans

3 pounds fresh green beans
5 cups water
1 (1/2-pound) ham hock
2 teaspoons salt
1/4 teaspoon pepper

Remove strings from beans and cut beans into 2-inch pieces. Wash thoroughly.

Pour water into a Dutch oven; add ham hock, and bring to a boil. Reduce heat, and simmer 1 hour. Add beans, salt, and pepper; cook 30 minutes or until tender. Yield: 10 to 12 servings.

Shenandoah Apple Juice Shrub

1 quart apple juice, chilled
Lime sherbet
Fresh mint (optional)

Pour apple juice into 4 large mugs or glasses. Top each with a generous scoop of sherbet. Garnish with a sprig of fresh mint, if desired. Yield: 4 servings.

Note: Cranberry juice or any other fruit juice or sherbet can be substituted for a refreshing drink.

Giblet Gravy

3 cups water
1 teaspoon salt
Giblets from 1 turkey
Turkey neck
1 medium onion, chopped (optional)
1 cup chopped celery (optional)
1/2 teaspoon poultry seasoning (optional)
6 tablespoons all-purpose flour
Salt and pepper

Combine 3 cups water and salt in a medium saucepan; bring to a boil. Add giblets and turkey neck; reduce heat. Cover and simmer 15 minutes. Remove liver, and continue simmering about 1-1/2 hours or until tender. Remove meat from broth, discarding neck; chop giblets, and return to broth.

If desired, add onion, celery, and poultry seasoning to broth mixture. Cook until vegetables are tender.

Dissolve flour in a small amount of water, mixing to form a smooth paste; stir into broth. Cook, stirring constantly, until thickened and bubbly. Season to taste with salt and pepper. Yield: about 3 cups.

Ambrosia Pie

2/3 cup sugar
1/4 cup cornstarch
1/2 teaspoon salt
3 cups milk
4 egg yolks, well beaten
2 tablespoons butter or margarine, softened
1 tablespoon plus 1 teaspoon vanilla extract
1 cup flaked coconut
1 baked 9-inch pastry shell
1/2 pint whipping cream
1/4 cup powdered sugar
1/4 cup flaked coconut, toasted
Mandarin orange sections

Combine sugar, cornstarch, and salt in a large saucepan; mix well. Combine milk and egg yolks, mixing well; stir into sugar mixture. Cook over medium heat; stirring constantly, until mixture thickens and boils; boil 1 minute, stirring constantly. Remove from heat; add butter, vanilla, and 1 cup coconut. Let cool, and spoon into pastry shell.

Whip cream until slightly thickened; add powdered sugar, beating until light and fluffy. Spread over pie filling; sprinkle with toasted coconut, and garnish with mandarin orange sections. Yield: one 9-inch pie.

Virginia Corn Relish

1/2 cup vinegar
1/2 cup sugar
1/2 teaspoon salt
1/2 teaspoon celery seeds
1/4 teaspoon mustard seeds
1/4 teaspoon hot sauce
1 (12-ounce) can whole kernel corn, undrained
2 tablespoons chopped green pepper
1 tablespoon instant minced onion
1 tablespoon chopped pimiento

Combine vinegar, sugar, salt, celery seeds, mustard seeds, and hot sauce in a medium saucepan; mix well. Bring to a boil; continue boiling 2 minutes or until sugar dissolves. Remove from heat, and add remaining ingredients; let cool. Refrigerate in airtight container for 2 days before serving to allow flavors to blend. Yield: 10 to 12 servings.

Fresh Cranberry Sauce

1 pound fresh cranberries
2 cups sugar
2 cups water
2 tablespoons grated orange rind

Carefully sort and wash cranberries. Combine cranberries, sugar, and water in a saucepan; cook about 10 minutes or until all berries burst. Add orange rind, and mash slightly. Yield: about 3 cups.

This oval table laden with elaborate concoctions—just the kind of spread every hungry traveler hopes to find—was drawn for The Court and Country Cook, *published in England in 1702. As the original engraver noted in the lower right corner of the picture, it was meant to embellish "the last page," and so it does.*